SENT, NOT SILENT

Kingdom Social Ethics For Engaging The World With Truth And Confidence

Dr. Jean Héder Petit-Frère

Dedication

This book is dedicated to a generation of believers who know they were created for more than silence.

It is for those who have felt the tension between their faith and the world around them, for those who have wrestled with hard questions, stood in places where truth was not welcomed, and still refused to let go of what they know God has placed inside them.

It is for the sons and daughters of the Kingdom who are rising above fear, confusion, and compromise, choosing instead to stand, to speak, and to engage.

And it is for every believer who has ever asked, *How do I live my faith boldly in a world that challenges it?*

This book is for you.

Acknowledgments

I express thanks first to God, the source of light, truth, and understanding.

Every conviction expressed on these pages flows from His revelation and from the burden of seeing His people walk with clarity and confidence.

To the leaders and members of the ministry, your questions, your growth, and your journey have helped reveal a pressing need:

Not simply to believe, but to understand, to think, and to express that faith with clarity.

To the Body of Christ, this book is written as a call, not to argue, but to awaken.

An awakening to the necessity of:

- thinking clearly
- knowing what we believe
- and expressing it with conviction in the world we live in

This is not the work of one moment but the fruit of a journey and a growing burden, so that the light we carry would no longer remain hidden but be understood, expressed, and lived.

Who This Book Is For

This book is not written for those who want to remain passive. It is written for believers who refuse to hide their faith, those who want to understand what they believe and desire to engage the world without losing who they are in Christ.

It is for the professional navigating a secular workplace with wisdom and courage. It is for the student encountering ideas that challenge their convictions. It is for the leader who seeks to influence systems rather than simply survive within them. And it is for the believer who is tired of silence and ready to make an impact.

If you are satisfied with a faith that remains private, a Christianity that stays comfortable, or a life that avoids difficult conversations, this book will likely unsettle you.

But if you are ready to think clearly, stand confidently, and engage intentionally, then this book will serve as a tool to strengthen and equip you.

Author's Note

This book was not written from theory alone. It grew out of years of observation, tension, and a deep burden in my heart.

Over time, I have watched many believers who are strong in worship, passionate in church, and sincere in their love for God, yet remain silent in the world around them, not because they do not believe, but because they often lack the clarity, confidence, and understanding needed to speak with strength.

I have seen genuine Christians struggle to explain what they believe, withdraw from important conversations, and feel intimidated in places they were actually called to influence.

This led me to a question I could not ignore: *Why are those who carry the light so often uncomfortable in the very places where they were sent to shine?*

This book is my response to that question.

It is not written to condemn, but to awaken. Not to criticize, but to equip.

My prayer is that as you read, you will not only grow in understanding, but also become more confident, more grounded, and more engaged.

The world does not need Christians who are quieter. It needs Christians who are clearer.

Introduction

Many believers today live with a growing tension.

They love God. They believe in Jesus. They are committed to their faith. Yet when they find themselves in a world that questions what they believe, challenges their values, and pushes against their convictions, they often hesitate.

It is not because they do not care. It is often because they are unsure how to respond.

So they remain silent. They avoid hard conversations. They stay in environments where their faith feels safe and unchallenged.

Over time, something subtle begins to happen: faith becomes private rather than influential. But that was never the intention of Jesus.

Jesus did not call His followers to withdraw from the world. He called them to engage it. He did not say to hide their light. He said, *"You are the light of the world."*

Light is not meant to be hidden. It is meant to be seen.

The Central Problem

The greatest issue today is not simply that darkness is increasing. The deeper issue is that many of those who are called to be light lack clarity, confidence, and understanding. When identity is uncertain, engagement feels dangerous, and silence begins to feel like the safer option.

The Purpose Of This Book

This book was written to help restore clarity, confidence, conviction, and competence.

It is meant to help you know what you believe, stand without intimidation, remain firm in your convictions, and engage the world with wisdom and effectiveness.

As you read, my hope is that you will learn to understand your identity in Christ more deeply, explain your faith more clearly, engage opposing views without fear, and apply your beliefs in real-world situations with courage and wisdom.

This Is Not Just a book; it is a Call

This book is a call to move from silence to speech, from avoidance to engagement, and from private belief to public influence. You were never meant to blend in, stay quiet, or live on the sidelines.

You were sent.

And it is time to live like it.

I can also do a second pass that makes it sound even more like a published Christian book with a stronger poetic and devotional tone.

Contents

Chapter 1: The Fear Of Darkness

Why Light Has Become Uncomfortable in the World It Was Sent to Illuminate

Sometimes, a believer's discomfort is rooted in inner uncertainty rather than the world around them. We may love God sincerely and still feel hesitant when faith must leave the comfort of agreement and enter the tension of real life.

This chapter brings that hidden struggle into the open. It invites us to look honestly at the places where fear has silenced us and to allow Christ to restore the confidence that belongs to those who know who they are in Him.

There is a silent crisis in the Body of Christ today. It is not a lack of churches. It is not a lack of messages. Believers are not lacking.

It is a lack of confidence in identity, and, as a result, a growing fear of engagement.

We were called light. Yet many who claim to be light are deeply uncomfortable in darkness. And that contradiction must be confronted.

This contradiction reaches into how we live, how we speak, how we respond, and sometimes how we retreat. When a believer begins to fear the very environment he was called to influence, something sacred has been forgotten.

Somewhere between confession and confrontation, between church and culture, and between worship and witness, a fracture begins to form. That fracture is not always visible at first, but over time, it affects the courage of the soul.

Light Was Never Meant to Hide

Jesus made a statement so simple that many have overlooked its weight:
"You are the light of the world. A city that is set on a hill cannot be hidden.", Matthew 5:14

Notice, He did not say, "You will become light." He said, "You are."

Light is not something we strive to be. It is an integral part of our identity.

But here is the tension:

- If we are light, why do we avoid dark places?
- If we are light, why do we feel threatened by opposing views?
- If we are light, why do we retreat instead of advance?

The answer is uncomfortable, but necessary: many believers are positionally light but functionally uncertain. And uncertainty produces fear.

This is where many sincere believers quietly struggle. They know the language of faith, but they have not fully settled into the weight of spiritual identity. They believe what God has said, but when resistance appears, insecurity begins to whisper.

In those moments, darkness seems larger than it is, not because darkness has grown stronger, but because identity has not grown deeper.

Scripture reminds us:

"The light shines in the darkness, and the darkness did not comprehend it." (John 1:5, NKJV)

Darkness has never had the final word over light. The problem is not that darkness is too strong. The problem is that too many believers have underestimated what God has already placed within them.

When Light Forgets What It Is

Darkness has never been a threat to light. Light does not fight darkness. Light simply appears, and darkness disappears.

The problem today is not the presence of darkness; it is the hesitation of light.

Many believers:

- Avoid conversations with people who think differently
- Stay silent in environments where truth is needed
- Withdraw from spaces where influence is required

Not because they don't care, but because they are not sure they can stand.

And that reveals something deeper: fear of darkness is often a sign of unresolved identity.

This is why fear in engagement should not only be managed, but it must be understood.

A believer may appear quiet, cautious, or reserved while something deeper is happening beneath the surface. Sometimes silence is not wisdom. Sometimes it is exhaustion. Sometimes it is insecurity. Sometimes it is the hidden fear that, if our faith is truly tested, we may not know how to carry it with peace.

But the Lord does not shame us for that weakness. He invites us to bring it into His light. He does not expose us to condemn us; He reveals us so He can heal us.

What we are willing to face honestly, He is willing to strengthen faithfully.

The Comfort of the Bubble

It is easier to be bold among people who already agree with you. It is easier to sound strong in environments where:

- Everyone speaks your language
- Everyone shares your beliefs
- Everyone affirms your convictions

But that is not where light is tested.

A lamp does not prove its usefulness in daylight. It proves its value in the night.

And yet, many believers have built environments where:

- They are constantly affirmed
- Rarely challenged
- Never required to explain what they believe

This creates a dangerous illusion, the illusion of strength without the reality of influence.

There is a kind of comfort that quietly weakens us. It feels safe, spiritual, and even healthy on the surface, yet it can leave us unprepared for the world we are actually called to enter. We become fluent in familiar language but fragile in unfamiliar spaces. We learn how to speak where there is no resistance, but not how to remain steady where truth must be carried with wisdom.

Comfort is not evil, but when comfort becomes our shelter from assignment, it begins to cost us more than we realize. God does not mature us only in places of agreement. He also matures us where discernment, patience, courage, and clarity are required.

Jesus: Light without Fear

Jesus did not avoid darkness. He walked directly into it. He sat with tax collectors. He spoke with sinners. He engaged skeptics. He confronted religious hypocrisy.

And yet, He was never:

- Contaminated
- Intimidated
- Confused

Why? Because his identity was never in question.

Jesus did not become light when He entered darkness; He brought light because He knew who He was.

This is the model we have been given:

- Not isolation
- Not compromise
- But confident engagement

What makes the life of Jesus so compelling is not only His holiness but also His steadiness. He was not anxious in broken spaces. He was not confused by the presence of confusion. He did not lose Himself in the middle of human need, human rebellion, or human contradiction. He entered those spaces carrying something deeper than reaction. He carried the settled presence of the Father.

This is why His example still speaks so powerfully to us. He shows us that spiritual maturity is not proven by how far we stay from darkness, but by how clearly we carry the light of God within it. His life teaches us that holiness and presence do not oppose one another. In Christ, they walk together.

"For the Son of Man has come to seek and to save that which was lost" (Luke 19:10, NKJV). Jesus did not move toward darkness to be shaped by it, but to rescue those trapped within it. That same redemptive pattern still shapes our calling today.

Fear Reveals a Gap

Let us be honest.

When a believer says, "I don't like being around people like that," or "I'd rather not get into those conversations," or "I just stay in my lane," it often sounds like wisdom.

But many times, it is avoidance disguised as maturity.

Because if your faith cannot stand in conversation, it will not stand in confrontation. And if it cannot stand in confrontation, it will not influence culture.

This is a painful truth, but a necessary one. There are times when what we call discernment is actually self-protection. There are times when what we call peace is really avoidance. There are times when what we call staying focused is actually shrinking back from the assignment to represent Christ where it matters most.

Of course, not every conversation is wise, and not every environment is healthy. Yet the larger issue remains: if our spiritual life only works where there is safety, then something in our foundation still needs strengthening. Mature faith does not depend on perfect surroundings. It carries conviction even when the surroundings are imperfect.

The Assignment of Light

Jesus did not say, "You are the light of the church." He said, "You are the light of the world."

That means:

- The marketplace
- Systems
- Conversations
- Ideologies
- Broken environments

Light has an assignment. And that assignment is not comfort, it is impact.

This is where the call of Christ becomes beautifully demanding. He does not define us only by what we avoid, but by what we carry. He sends us into ordinary places with holy purpose. The office, the classroom, the neighborhood, the family tension, the difficult conversation, the public space, the private burden of another person—none of these are outside the reach of divine assignment.

The believer is not merely passing through the world trying to remain untouched. The believer is sent through the world to bear witness. That changes everything. It changes how we see pressure. It changes how we see people. It changes how we see opportunity.

As 2 Corinthians 5:20 says, "Now then, we are ambassadors for Christ" (NKJV). An ambassador does not hide from the environment he is sent to. He represents another kingdom within it.

The Real Issue Is Not Darkness

Darkness is doing what darkness does.

The real question is: why is light not doing what it was created to do?

The answer is not more isolation. The answer is not louder preaching within safe spaces.

The answer is a return to identity.

Because when identity is clear:

- Fear loses its grip
- Confidence rises
- Engagement becomes natural

Identity changes the emotional temperature of the believer. When identity is unsettled, everything feels threatening. Questions feel personal. Opposition feels crushing. Differences feel destabilizing. But when identity is rooted in Christ, the soul no longer lives in survival mode. It becomes calm enough to listen, strong enough to stand, and humble enough to speak truth without fear.

This is why the restoration of identity is not a side issue. It is central. A believer who knows he belongs to Christ, who knows he is loved by the Father, and who knows the Spirit of God dwells within him will not need constant approval from the world around him. He will be able to remain present without losing himself.

What Happens When Identity Is Restored

When a believer truly understands who they are:

- They no longer avoid difficult conversations
- They no longer feel inferior in intellectual spaces
- They no longer retreat from opposing views

Instead:

- They listen without fear
- They speak with clarity
- They stand with conviction

Not to win arguments, but to reveal truth.

That is the beauty of restored identity: it does not make a person louder for the sake of being noticed. It makes a person steadier for the sake of being useful. The believer no longer enters conversations desperate to prove worth. He enters as one who has already been secured by grace. From that place, his words become cleaner, his spirit becomes calmer, and his witness becomes more credible.

There is also compassion in this kind of strength. When identity is settled, we no longer need to treat every disagreement as a threat. We can speak firmly without cruelty. We can disagree without panic. We can remain anchored without becoming harsh. This is the kind of witness the world rarely forgets.

"But sanctify the Lord God in your hearts, and always be ready to give a defense to everyone who asks you a reason for the hope that is in you, with meekness and fear" (1 Peter 3:15, NKJV). Notice the balance—readiness, reason, meekness, and reverence. This is not fearful silence, nor is it aggressive pride. It is mature clarity.

A Necessary Shift

The Church must shift from:

1. Avoidance → Engagement
2. Silence → Articulation
3. Insecurity → Identity

Because the world is not waiting for louder Christians. It is waiting for clearer ones.

And clarity does not begin on a stage. It begins in the hidden place where the believer lets God settle what fear has unsettled. It begins when we stop excusing spiritual hesitation and start inviting the Lord to strengthen what is weak within us. It begins when we remember that we were not saved merely to survive darkness, but to shine within it.

The call of this chapter is not simply to do more. It is to become more settled in Christ. From that place, engagement stops feeling like a burden and starts feeling like obedience. The believer begins to realize that he does not enter dark places alone. He enters carrying the presence, truth, and authority of the One who sent him.

Points to Ponder

1. Where do I feel uncomfortable engaging people with different beliefs?
2. Is my silence rooted in wisdom, or insecurity?
3. Do I truly understand why I believe what I believe?
4. Am I functioning as light, or only identified as light?
5. Have I mistaken comfort for spiritual maturity?
6. What environments reveal where my identity needs strengthening?

7.   In what ways might God be inviting me to stop retreating and begin representing Him with greater peace and courage?

Call to Action

This week, intentionally engage in one conversation you would normally avoid.

Not to argue. Not to prove a point. But to:

- Listen
- Understand
- Respond with clarity and grace

Growth begins where comfort ends.

Before that conversation happens, spend time in prayer and remind yourself of who you are in Christ. Do not enter the moment trying to impress anyone. Enter it surrendered, steady, and aware that your role is not to force results, but to faithfully represent Jesus.

Afterward, reflect honestly: Where did fear try to rise? Where did grace help you remain present? Let the experience teach you, not intimidate you.

Declaration

I am the light of the world. I do not fear darkness because darkness cannot overcome light. My identity is secure in Christ.

I will not withdraw, I will engage.

I carry truth with clarity, conviction, and grace. Through me, light will shine in every space I enter.

I will not let insecurity silence what God has placed within me.

I am not called to hide in safe places, but to walk faithfully in the places where God has sent me.

The Spirit of God within me is greater than the fear around me.

Prayer

Father,

Thank you for calling me light. Forgive me for the times I have hidden, withdrawn, or remained silent out of fear.

Strengthen my identity in You. Give me clarity in what I believe and boldness to express it. Teach me to engage the world without losing my convictions.

Help me reflect Christ in every conversation, every environment, and every opportunity.

Let my life not only declare truth but also demonstrate it.

In Jesus' name, Amen.

Chapter 2: Belief Without Understanding

Why Many Christians Believe Deeply but Cannot Explain Clearly

This chapter touches a quiet weakness many believers carry with sincerity, not rebellion. They love Jesus, trust Him, worship Him, and remain devoted to Him, yet when their faith is examined in conversation, they often feel exposed. Not because their faith is false, but because it has not been trained to speak with clarity.

There is a difference between possessing faith and being able to express it well. God desires both. He is honored not only by our devotion in private but also by our readiness to speak truth wisely when the moment requires it.

There is a dangerous gap in the lives of many believers. It is the gap between faith and understanding. Many truly believe in Jesus. They love Him. They worship Him. They are committed to Him. But when asked a simple question, *"Why do you believe?"*, they struggle to answer. Not because they are insincere, but because they have never been trained to think through their faith.

That gap is more serious than it first appears. A believer may remain emotionally strong for a while, yet still become unstable when confronted by persistent questions, intellectual pressure, or cultural skepticism. What is not understood clearly often becomes difficult to communicate faithfully. And what cannot be communicated faithfully is often carried timidly.

This is why understanding matters. It does not replace faith; it strengthens faith so that belief is no longer silent when it should be expressed.

Sincerity Is Not the Same as Clarity

Sincerity is powerful, but it is not enough. A person can be:

- Deeply sincere
- Emotionally connected
- Spiritually active

…and still be unable to articulate their beliefs.

In a world that constantly asks questions, challenges ideas, and tests convictions, this creates a serious problem. Because what you cannot explain, you will eventually struggle to defend.

Sincerity can keep the heart warm, but clarity helps the mind remain steady. Many believers were taught how to feel deeply in worship, but not always how to think carefully in conversation. They know the presence of God, but they do not always know how to describe the hope that lives within them.

This leaves them vulnerable in ordinary moments, at work, at school, in friendships, and in public discussions, when a simple question reveals a deeper lack of preparation.

The Lord does not call us to choose between spiritual fire and spiritual understanding. He calls us into a faith that burns and thinks, a faith that feels and knows, a faith that can worship sincerely and answer honestly.

The Question Most Christians Fear

Let's be honest. Many believers are uncomfortable when conversations shift from *"I feel God..."* to *"Why is that true?"* Because feelings are personal. But truth demands explanation.

Questions like these are no longer rare:

- Why Jesus and not another path?
- Why does God allow suffering?
- Why should anyone believe the Bible?
- Isn't Christianity just one option among many?

These are everyday conversations. And yet many believers:

- Avoid them
- Redirect them
- Or shut down entirely

Not because the answers do not exist, but because they have never been equipped with them.

This is where many Christians feel the tension of modern life. In previous generations, some beliefs were assumed or socially reinforced. Today, almost everything is questioned by some, which feels threatening. But in another sense, it is an invitation. Questions can become open doors. Honest challenges can become moments of witness. Yet that can only happen when the believer is willing to grow beyond vague language and into thoughtful understanding.

We should not be ashamed that people ask questions. Questions do not automatically signal hostility. Sometimes they reveal pain. Sometimes confusion. Sometimes sincere searching. Sometimes, there is disappointment with distorted religion. When we learn to hear the question beneath the question, we become less defensive and more discerning. That is part of mature witness.

A Faith That Cannot Be Explained Becomes Fragile.

When belief is not supported by understanding:

- Doubt grows easily
- Confidence weakens quickly
- Influence disappears silently

This is why some believers:

- Start strong but fade over time
- Believe in church but struggle in the marketplace
- Sound confident in worship but uncertain in conversation

Because their faith was never built to withstand questions.

Fragile faith is not always weak because it lacks passion. Often, it is weak because it lacks roots. A tree may appear alive above the ground, yet if its roots are shallow, strong winds will reveal what calm seasons concealed. In the same way, a believer may sound spiritually alive until pressure comes in the form of questions, mockery, contradiction, or intellectual challenge. Then what seemed secure begins to shake.

Scripture gives us a different picture of what God desires. Colossians 2:7 speaks of being *"rooted and built up in Him and established in the faith"* (NKJV). Rooted faith is not frightened by examination. It may not know every answer instantly, but it is stable enough to keep seeking, learning, and standing.

God Never Asked for Blind Faith

Contrary to popular belief, Christianity is not anti-thinking. God does not say, *"Turn off your mind and just believe."* In fact, Scripture consistently calls for understanding.

- *"Come now, and let us reason together," says the Lord.* , Isaiah 1:18
- *"Always be ready to give a defense… for the hope that is in you."* 1 Peter 3:15

God invites reasoning. God expects articulation. God desires a faith that is not only experienced but also understood.

This matters deeply because many believers, without meaning to, have inherited a false tension between spirituality and thoughtfulness. They have been made to feel that deep thinking threatens simple faith, when in reality, surrendered thinking can deepen faith. God created the mind as well as the heart. He is not intimidated by inquiry, and He does not need ignorance to protect truth.

Truth remains truth even when examined closely.

Christian faith is not built on empty emotion, nor on a demand for mental silence. It is rooted in the person of Christ, the witness of Scripture, the transforming work of the Spirit, and the coherence of God's truth across life itself. The believer does not need to fear the life of the mind. He simply needs to keep it yielded to God.

Jesus: Clear, Intelligent, and Unshaken

Jesus did not avoid questions. He welcomed them, answered them, turned them around, and used them to reveal the truth.

When challenged by:

- Pharisees
- Skeptics
- Lawyers
- Crowds

Jesus was never intimidated. Why? Because truth does not panic under pressure.

Jesus knew what He believed. He knew who He was. He knew how to communicate with wisdom. This is our model, not merely passion, but articulated truth.

There is something deeply beautiful about the way Jesus spoke. He was never hurried by human pressure. He was never cornered by manipulation. He was never impressed by intellectual posturing. Sometimes, he answered directly. Sometimes, he asked a deeper question. Sometimes, he exposed the motives behind the question itself. In every case, He remained steady. His clarity flowed from union with the Father, not from anxiety about public opinion.

This is important for us. Christian clarity is not meant to sound arrogant or combative. In Jesus, clarity was joined with wisdom, timing, and discernment. He did not answer merely to win. He answered to reveal. He spoke in ways that uncovered hearts, invited reflection, and pointed people back to truth.

Luke 2:47 says that those who heard Him were *"astonished at His understanding and answers"* (NKJV). Even from a young age, there was evidence that truth, when deeply formed, can be spoken with unusual clarity and weight.

The Church Has Emphasized Experience More Than Explanation

In many Christian spaces, people are taught how to:

- Pray
- Worship
- Serve
- Feel the presence of God

But not always how to:

- Think clearly
- Explain biblical truth
- Respond to objections
- Understand difficult questions

So believers grow emotionally, yet remain intellectually unprepared. And when they face a world that demands explanation, they feel exposed.

This is not a condemnation of spiritual experience. Real encounters with God matter. Worship matters. Prayer matters. Service matters. But if believers are formed only devotionally and not also strengthened in understanding, they may become spiritually sincere yet conversationally unready. That imbalance leaves them with language for church settings, but not always for real-world engagement.

The answer is not to reduce spiritual life to debate or information. The answer is to bring formation into balance. The believer should be able to pray deeply, love well, read Scripture faithfully, and also communicate the truth of the gospel with humble coherence.

These things belong together. They are not enemies.

Why This Matters More Than Ever

We live in an age of:

- Constant information
- Competing worldviews
- Public skepticism
- Intellectual pressure

This means believers can no longer afford to live on inherited language alone. It is no longer enough to say, *"This is just what I grew up believing.*" Faith must become personally understood, not just traditionally received.

This generation is surrounded by voices. Some are persuasive. Some are intelligent. Some are wounded. Some are deceptive. Many speak with confidence, even when they lack truth. In such an environment, borrowed convictions will not carry a believer very far. What was merely inherited must become examined, embraced, and personally grounded.

Otherwise, the soul may repeat Christian language while inwardly drifting into uncertainty.

This is one reason spiritual maturity now requires intentional depth. A believer does not need to become a scholar to become clear. But he must become rooted enough to know what he believes, why he believes it, and how to express it in a way that is truthful, understandable, and human.

Faith Must Mature Beyond Emotion

Emotions matter. Experience matters. But faith cannot remain there, because emotions fluctuate and experiences vary.

Truth must become anchored in understanding. Otherwise, when feelings fade, confidence goes with them.

This does not mean emotion is shallow. God often touches us deeply through worship, conviction, comfort, joy, and tears. But emotion was never meant to be the whole structure of faith. It can awaken us, but it cannot carry the entire weight of conviction by itself. Mature faith learns how to bless God on days of emotional fire and on days of emotional quiet, because its foundation is not merely what it feels, but what it knows to be true.

Paul's words to Timothy carry this kind of settled confidence: *"For I know whom I have believed and am persuaded that He is able to keep what I have committed to Him"* (2 Timothy 1:12, NKJV). Notice the language, not only feeling, but knowing; not only devotion, but persuasion. This is the kind of maturity that remains when circumstances shift.

Understanding Builds Confidence

When you understand your faith, you become:

- Less intimidated
- More stable
- More articulate
- More useful in conversation

Understanding gives structure to conviction. It helps you move from *"I believe"* to *"This is why I believe."* And that changes everything.

Confidence born of understanding is different from loudness. It is quieter, steadier, and more durable. It does not need to dominate a conversation to remain present in it. It can listen without collapsing. It can answer without panic. It can admit what it does not yet know without feeling defeated. That is one of the hidden strengths of mature faith; it is secure enough to keep learning.

The believer who understands more clearly becomes more useful to others. Friends, coworkers, younger believers, searching souls, and even skeptics may all encounter someone whose words carry peace because they come from a conviction that has been thoughtfully formed. Clarity is not only for self-protection. It is also for service.

Knowing why you believe deepens how you believe. Understanding is not only for defending faith. It is also for deepening faith.

When you begin to understand:

- Why Jesus is trustworthy
- Why Scripture is reliable
- Why truth matters

Your relationship with God becomes more grounded.

Not colder, but stronger.

A faith that understands more deeply often becomes more tender, not less. The more clearly we see the beauty of Christ, the coherence of Scripture, the wisdom of God, and the power of the gospel, the more worship deepens with substance. Insight does not have to dry out devotion. In a healthy spiritual life, insight can make devotion richer, steadier, and more reverent.

It is one thing to sing about grace. It is another thing to understand what grace has done, why it was necessary, and how deeply it reveals the heart of God. That kind of understanding does not weaken worship. It gives worship roots.

What the Church Must Recover

The Church must disciple believers not only in:

- Passion
- Devotion
- Spiritual activity

but also in:

- Reasoning
- Biblical literacy
- Articulation
- Clarity

Because if the Church produces believers who feel deeply but cannot explain clearly, then it has not fully prepared them for the world.

This recovery is urgent. Churches must become places where believers are not only inspired but also formed; not only moved but also equipped. There must be room for questions, room for honest learning, room for difficult topics, room for patient explanation, and room for growth without shame.

The goal is not to create argumentative Christians. The goal is to form clear, grounded, humble disciples of Jesus.

Acts 18:24 describes Apollos as *"an eloquent man and mighty in the Scriptures"* (NKJV). That phrase is striking. He was not merely enthusiastic. He was mighty in the Scriptures.

The Church needs believers whose love for God is joined to depth in the Word.

A Believer Should Be Able to Say Something Meaningful

Not everyone will be a theologian. Not everyone will debate publicly. But every believer should be able to explain:

- Why Jesus matters to them
- What the gospel means
- Why they trust Scripture
- Why do they have hope

Not perfectly, but clearly.

This is not optional maturity. It is part of faithful representation.

The world does not require every Christian to become an expert, but it should be able to encounter believers who can speak meaningfully about the hope they carry. Even a simple explanation, if it is honest and clear, can become powerful. Many lives are not changed by polished speeches, but by truthful words spoken with humility and conviction.

The important thing is not sounding impressive. It is becoming understandable.

Sometimes the clearest witness is the believer who can say, with sincerity and coherence, who Christ is, what He has done, and why that truth has become unshakable in the heart.

The Goal Is Not to Win Arguments

The goal is not:

- To sound smart
- To defeat people intellectually
- To dominate conversations

The goal is to represent truth in a way that invites others to consider it.

Because people are not changed by arguments alone. They are changed by:

- Truth
- Clarity
- Love expressed through understanding

This protects us from a different danger. Some people seek understanding only to gain superiority, to win verbal battles, or to appear intellectually secure. But that is not the spirit of Christ. Christian understanding should produce humility, not pride. The more we know the truth, the more carefully we should carry it.

The purpose of explanation is not self-exaltation. It is a faithful witness.

1 Peter 3:15 does not only tell us to be ready with an answer. It also tells us to answer *"with meekness and fear"* (NKJV), with gentleness and reverence. Clarity without humility can wound. But clarity carried with grace can open hearts.

A Necessary Upgrade

The Church must move from:

- Belief → Understanding
- Passion → Clarity
- Silence → Articulation

Because the world is not lacking opinions, it is lacking clear, grounded truth.

And that truth must live in real people, not only in sermons, books, and pulpits. It must live in believers whose convictions have been strengthened enough to enter conversations without fear. It must live in those who are still growing, yet no longer content to remain unformed.

This is the upgrade required in our time: not a colder Christianity, but a clearer one; not a harsher witness, but a wiser one; not less faith, but faith made stronger through understanding.

Points to Ponder

1. If someone asked me why I believe in Jesus, what would I say?
2. Do I rely more on feelings or understanding in my faith?
3. What questions about my faith am I currently unable to answer?
4. Am I intentionally growing in knowledge or only in experience?

5.   Have I mistaken spiritual sincerity for spiritual preparedness?
6.   Where do I feel most vulnerable when my faith is questioned?
7.   What part of my belief needs deeper study so my conviction can become clearer and steadier?

Call to Action

This week, take time to write down your answer to one question: "Why do I believe in Jesus?" Keep it simple. Keep it clear. Keep it honest. Then refine it until you can say it confidently in a conversation.

Also, choose one question about Christianity that has made you uncomfortable, and study it prayerfully. Look into Scripture. Take notes. Seek a sound biblical understanding. Do not study from panic, but from hunger.

Let this become the beginning of a stronger, clearer faith.

Declaration

My faith is not shallow. I grow in understanding daily. I know what I believe, and I am learning why I believe it.

I am not intimidated by questions. I am equipped to respond with clarity, wisdom, and grace. Through me, truth will be expressed with confidence.

I do not fear honest questions, because truth stands firm. My mind is submitted to God, and my faith is becoming clearer, stronger, and more deeply rooted. I will not remain silent through uncertainty; I will grow until I can represent Christ with peace and conviction.

Prayer

Father,

Thank You for the gift of faith. But I ask You now, take me deeper into understanding. Remove every fear I have of questions and challenges. Give me a hunger to know the truth, not just feel it.

Teach me how to think, how to explain, and how to represent You well. Let my faith be both alive in my heart and clear in my words.

Make me a voice of truth in a world full of confusion.

Lord, where my faith has been sincere but unformed, strengthen me. Where I have hidden behind silence because I did not know how to answer, teach me patiently. Give me a love for Your Word, a disciplined mind, and a humble spirit.

Help me not to chase knowledge for pride, but to seek understanding so I may know You more deeply and represent You more faithfully. Let my heart stay tender while my convictions grow strong. And when I am questioned, let me respond with truth, grace, steadiness, and peace.

In Jesus' name,

Amen.

Chapter 3: The Crisis Of Christian Identity

Why Insecure Believers Avoid a World They Were Sent to Transform

There are struggles in the believer's life that do not begin in public, but in the hidden chambers of the heart. A person can love God, serve faithfully, and still carry an inward uncertainty that affects every outward response.

This chapter exposes that hidden instability with honesty and grace. It reminds us that many forms of silence, withdrawal, and hesitation are not always rooted in wisdom. Sometimes they are rooted in an identity that has not yet fully rested in what God has spoken.

There is a deeper issue beneath fear, beneath silence, and beneath avoidance.

It is not a lack of opportunity. It is not a lack of truth. It is a lack of identity.

Because when identity is unclear, everything else becomes unstable.

Identity is not a small matter in the life of faith. It shapes how we endure pressure, how we interpret opposition, how we respond to challenges, and how we carry ourselves in spaces that do not affirm what we believe. When identity is unsteady, even ordinary resistance can feel larger than it really is. But when identity is rooted in God, the soul begins to stand differently.

The Root of Withdrawal Is Not Darkness, It Is Uncertainty

Christians are not withdrawing from the world because the world is too dark. They are withdrawing because they are not fully convinced of who they are in the light.

When identity is weak:

- Opposition feels threatening
- Questions feel intimidating
- Differences feel overwhelming

But when identity is strong:

- Opposition becomes engagement
- Questions become opportunities
- Differences become doors

The difference is not the environment. The difference is the person.

This is why two believers can face the same environment and respond in completely different ways. One withdraws; another remains steady. One feels threatened; another senses assignment. The difference is not always knowledge, gifting, or personality. Often, it is the depth of inward certainty. A settled believer does not pretend pressure is easy, but he is no longer defined by it.

Scripture says, *"The spirit of a man will sustain him in sickness, but who can bear a broken spirit?"* (Proverbs 18:14, NKJV). When the inner life is weakened, everything feels heavier. But when the inner life is strengthened by truth, the believer can endure more than he once thought possible.

The Orphan Mindset in the Believer

Many believers are saved, but still think like orphans. They:

- Love God
- Serve in church
- Participate in spiritual activities

…but internally:

- They feel unsure
- They feel inadequate
- They feel easily shaken

This is what we call the orphan mindset.

An orphan:

- Seeks approval
- Avoids rejection
- Fears being exposed

So when conversations become challenging, the orphan mindset says:

- "Stay quiet."
- "Don't say too much."
- "Protect yourself."

The orphan mindset is painful because it can exist beneath sincere devotion. A believer may pray, worship, and serve, and still carry internal patterns shaped by insecurity. He may know God as Savior, yet still struggle to rest in Him as Father. That gap creates tension in the soul. He begins to look outward for reassurance instead of inward to what God has already declared.

This is one reason some believers feel unusually fragile when challenged. They are not merely defending a position. Deep down, they feel as though they are defending their worth. And when worth feels unstable, silence begins to feel safer than engagement.

Sonship Produces Confidence

The Kingdom does not operate on orphanhood; it operates on sonship.

"For you did not receive the spirit of bondage again to fear, but you received the Spirit of adoption…", Romans 8:15

A son knows:

- Who does he belong to
- What he carries
- Where he stands

So a son:

- Does not shrink back
- Does not panic under pressure
- Does not lose himself in opposing environments

Because his identity is not defined by the room, it is defined by the Father.

This is the healing truth the believer must return to again and again: we do not build our identity from the reactions of people around us. We receive it from the Father who has already spoken. Sonship gives stability where insecurity once ruled. It teaches the heart to stop searching for permission to stand in what God has already given.

"Behold what manner of love the Father has bestowed on us, that we should be called children of God!" (1 John 3:1, NKJV)

This is not symbolic language. It is relational truth. To know that we are His is to gain a foundation deeper than approval, stronger than rejection, and steadier than circumstance.

Jesus: The Model of Secure Identity

Before Jesus did anything publicly, something was established privately:

"This is My beloved Son, in whom I am well pleased.", Matthew 3:17

Notice: this affirmation came before:

- Miracles
- Teaching
- Ministry impact

Why? Because identity must be established before engagement begins.

Jesus did not enter the world trying to prove who He was. He entered the world knowing who He was.

That is why:

- He could stand before Pharisees without intimidation
- He could speak the truth without hesitation
- He could engage sinners without compromise

There is a deep tenderness in this pattern. The Father affirmed the Son before public works, before visible fruit, and before any human recognition. That means identity in God is not earned through performance. It is received in a relationship. Jesus ministered from belovedness, not for belovedness.

That distinction changes everything.

Many believers exhaust themselves trying to prove spiritually what God is inviting them to receive relationally. But when the heart truly accepts the Father's voice, striving begins to loosen its grip. We no longer enter spaces desperate to establish ourselves. We enter them carrying what heaven has already spoken.

When Identity Is Missing, Performance Takes Over

If you do not know who you are, you will try to prove who you are. And this leads to:

- Overcompensation

- Silence
- Inconsistency

Some believers become aggressive and defensive, while others become passive and withdrawn. But both are signs of the same issue: identity is not settled.

This is important to understand because insecurity does not always look timid. Sometimes it becomes loud. Sometimes it becomes sharp, reactive, or overly forceful. Other times, it becomes quiet, hesitant, and evasive. But both extremes can come from the same root: a soul that has not yet found rest in who it is before God.

A settled identity does not need to perform for acceptance. It does not need to dominate a room or disappear from one. It carries a steadier strength. It can be calm without being weak and clear without being defensive.

Why Identity Affects Social Engagement

If a believer is unsure of their identity:

- They will avoid environments where they can be challenged
- They will stay around people who affirm them
- They will hesitate to engage different worldviews

Not because they lack truth, but because they lack confidence in carrying it.

This is where the practical cost of weak identity becomes visible. The believer may sincerely have truth, yet still fail to carry it into the very places where it is needed most. He remains in safe circles, familiar language, and low-risk environments, not always because God called him there, but because fear made those places feel manageable.

Yet the mission of Christ was never meant to remain trapped in comfort. Believers are called to bring light into tension, not merely admire light in safe places. Until identity is strengthened, engagement will continue to feel threatening instead of purposeful.

Zacchaeus Revisited: Identity Produces Action

When Jesus encountered Zacchaeus, something powerful happened. Zacchaeus did not just receive forgiveness. He experienced identity restoration. And immediately:

- His values changed
- His behavior changed
- His economic decisions changed

"I give half of my goods to the poor…"

"If I have taken anything… I restore it fourfold."

Zacchaeus did not need:

- A law
- A policy
- External pressure

His identity shift produced social transformation.

This is one of the clearest signs that identity is never merely internal language. When identity is restored, life begins to move in a different direction. Choices change. Priorities shift. Relationships are touched. What is hidden in the heart eventually becomes visible in conduct.

Luke 19 shows us that grace is not passive. When Jesus enters a life, He does not merely comfort the conscience. He reorders the person. Zacchaeus became evidence that transformation is strongest when it flows from within rather than being forced from without.

You cannot Transform What You Are Afraid Of

This must be said clearly: you cannot influence a world you are afraid to engage. And you will always fear what you feel inferior to.

Many believers:

- Feel intellectually inferior
- Feel socially inferior
- Feel culturally outmatched

So instead of stepping in, they step back.

Fear often hides behind more respectable language. It may call itself caution, wisdom, or discernment, yet underneath it may still be quiet inferiority. The believer assumes others are stronger, sharper, more informed, or more culturally secure, and this inward comparison begins to silence him before the conversation even starts.

But inferiority is not humility. Humility rests in God. Inferiority shrinks from people. One keeps the heart teachable. The other keeps the voice hidden. The Lord does not call us to arrogant engagement, but neither does He call us to fearful retreat.

Identity Removes Inferiority

When identity is secure:

- You do not feel less than anyone else
- You do not feel intimidated
- You do not feel the need to withdraw

You understand: "I am not here to compete with the world. I am here to bring something the world does not have."

That changes everything.

This is where spiritual confidence becomes holy and useful. The believer no longer enters a room trying to match the world on its terms. He enters carrying something the world cannot generate on its own: truth shaped by grace, conviction strengthened by love, and the presence of God in a human life.

That realization produces peace. You stop measuring your worth by the tone of the room. You stop reading opposition as proof that you do not belong there. You begin to understand that you were not sent because you are naturally impressive. You were sent because Christ in you is sufficient.

"You are of God, little children, and have overcome them, because He who is in you is greater than he who is in the world." (1 John 4:4, NKJV)

This is not motivational language. It is a spiritual reality.

The Church Must Rebuild Identity First

Before teaching believers how to:

- Engage culture
- Defend their faith
- Influence society

We must first establish who they are.

Because methods without identity create pressure. But identity produces:

- Confidence
- Stability
- Clarity

This is a pastoral issue as much as it is a theological one. Many believers do not need louder instructions first. They need deeper formation. They need to be reminded of who they are in Christ, what the cross secured, what adoption means, and what it looks like to live from acceptance rather than striving.

Training matters. Strategy matters. Understanding matters. But when these things are built on insecurity, they often become burdensome. When they are built on identity, they become life-giving. The order matters.

Identity must come first.

The Restoration of Identity

When identity is restored:

- Fear gives way to boldness
- Silence gives way to clarity
- Avoidance gives way to engagement

The believer no longer asks, "Can I survive in that environment?" He begins to ask, "What can I bring into that environment?"

That is the beautiful turning point of maturity. The mind shifts from self-preservation to Kingdom contribution. The believer stops reading every environment through the lens of threat and starts reading it through the lens of assignment. What once felt intimidating begins to look like an opportunity for witness, service, and truth.

Restored identity does not remove all discomfort, but it changes how discomfort is interpreted. The believer no longer assumes challenge means he should retreat. Sometimes, the challenge is simply the doorway into faithful presence.

A Turning Point

This is where everything begins to shift. The problem is not:

- The world is too dark
- The questions are too hard
- The opposition being too strong

The problem is that believers have not yet settled on who they are.

But once identity is established, everything changes.

This chapter is not an accusation. It is an invitation. It invites the believer to stop living beneath what the Father has already spoken. It calls us out of spiritual insecurity and into the confidence that belongs to those who know they are loved, called, and sent.

Once identity becomes settled, engagement no longer feels like trespassing. It begins to feel like obedience. The believer stands not because the world becomes easier, but because the heart becomes clearer.

Points to Ponder

1. Do I see myself as a son or daughter, or do I still operate from insecurity?
2. What environments make me feel intimidated, and why?
3. Am I avoiding engagement because I lack clarity, or because I lack confidence?
4. Has my identity in Christ truly been settled?
5. Where do I still look for human approval in ways that weaken my spiritual confidence?
6. What part of my life most clearly reveals whether I am living as a son or reacting like an orphan?
7. Have I been protecting myself from discomfort when God may actually be calling me into deeper maturity?

Call to Action

Take time this week to study Scriptures about your identity in Christ, especially Romans 8 and Ephesians 1–2. Write down:

- Who God says you are
- What he says you carry

Read those truths daily until they become your conviction.

As you do this, do not rush through the words. Sit with them prayerfully. Let them confront every lie you have believed about yourself. Read them aloud if necessary. Return to them when insecurity rises. Let Scripture become stronger in your heart than the voices that have kept you hesitant.

Declaration

I am a child of God. I am secure in my identity. I do not shrink back in the face of opposition.

I carry truth with confidence and clarity. I am not intimidated by the world; I am sent into it. Through me, God will bring light, truth, and transformation.

I do not live for approval, because I already belong to the Father. I reject every orphan mindset that teaches me to fear where God has called me to stand. My identity is rooted in Christ, and from that place I will live, speak, and engage with peace.

Prayer

Father,

Thank you for calling me your own. Deliver me from every mindset that keeps me thinking like an orphan. Establish my identity deeply in You. Remove every fear, every insecurity, and every sense of inferiority.

Teach me to walk as Your child, confident, grounded, and unshaken. Let my life reflect who I truly am in You. From this day forward, I will not withdraw. I will engage, represent, and transform.

Lord, heal every place in me where insecurity has spoken louder than Your truth. Silence every lie that has taught me to live as though I am abandoned, unqualified, or alone. Let the reality of Your love settle so deeply in me that I no longer need to prove myself before people. Teach me to carry myself with the quiet confidence of one who belongs to You.

Strengthen me in every environment where I have felt small, uncertain, or intimidated. Let Your voice become the strongest voice in my heart, and let my life reveal the peace, courage, and steadiness of true sonship.

In Jesus' name, Amen.

Chapter 4: Jesus Among Sinners (Not Separate From Them)

The Model We Were Given but Rarely Follow

There is something deeply revealing about the way Jesus moved through the world. He did not build His ministry around distance, safety, or image management. He moved with purity, but He also moved with nearness.

This chapter calls us to face a difficult question with honesty: have we confused spiritual caution with Christlike faithfulness? Many believers want to remain pure, but very few have learned how to remain pure while staying meaningfully present among those who are far from God. Yet this is exactly what Jesus modeled.

There is a version of Christianity that is widely practiced, but rarely examined. It is a version that:

- Stays close to believers
- Keeps distance from sinners
- Avoids uncomfortable environments

…and calls it wisdom or holiness.

But when placed side by side with the life of Jesus, it becomes difficult to defend.

Because Jesus did not model avoidance. He modeled engagement.

That contrast should not be rushed past. It exposes more than a method; it reveals a mindset. Somewhere along the way, many believers began to assume that distance was the safest proof of devotion. But the life of Jesus shows something richer and stronger. Real holiness is not proven only by what it avoids. It is also revealed by what it can enter without being corrupted and by who it can love without becoming compromised.

The Reputation of Jesus

At one point, Jesus was given a label: "This Man receives sinners and eats with them," Luke 15:2

This was not a compliment. It was criticism.

Religious leaders were uncomfortable with how freely Jesus interacted with people they considered:

- Unclean
- Corrupt
- Morally compromised

And yet, that was exactly where Jesus chose to be.

This matters because criticism often reveals what religion does not understand. The Pharisees thought nearness to sinners was evidence of looseness. In reality, it was evidence of love, confidence, and mission. Jesus did not move toward broken people because He had weak standards. He moved toward them because He carried a strong redemptive purpose. He was not looking for approval from the religious crowd. He was fulfilling the heart of the Father.

"For the Son of Man has come to seek and to save that which was lost." (Luke 19:10, NKJV)

That verse does not describe a Savior waiting at a distance. It describes one who moves toward what is lost with intention, compassion, and authority.

Presence Is the First Step to Influence

You cannot influence what you refuse to be present in. This is where many believers miss it.

They want:

- Impact without proximity
- Transformation without interaction
- Influence without engagement

But Jesus understood something clearly: presence precedes transformation.

He did not shout truth from a distance. He brought truth into proximity.

This is one of the simplest and most overlooked realities of ministry. Influence usually begins before words are fully spoken. It begins with presence, with willingness, with entering the human space where fear, pain, confusion, and sin are already at work. We often want results while remaining untouched by inconvenience.

But Jesus stepped into rooms, homes, tensions, and relationships. He allowed truth to draw near enough to be felt.

Many lives remain unchanged not because truth is absent, but because truth has remained too far away to be trusted. Presence does not replace truth. It prepares the ground where truth can be received.

The Table Was His Strategy

Jesus often met people at the table. Meals were not random; they were intentional.

At the table:

- Conversations happen
- Walls come down
- Trust is built

This is why He:

- Dined with tax collectors
- Sat with sinners
- Engaged people others rejected

The table became a place where:

- Truth was introduced
- Hearts were opened
- Lives were changed

There is a quiet beauty in this. Jesus understood that shared space softens defensiveness. A table is not merely furniture; it is a setting where people become visible, where masks grow thinner, where stories emerge, and where the heart can begin to open. What religion may reject from afar, love often reaches through simple closeness.

For many believers, the table still matters. It may not always be a literal meal, but it will often look like intentional space, moments where a person feels seen rather than managed, heard rather than dismissed, welcomed rather than judged from a distance. Ministry becomes more human when presence becomes intentional.

Zacchaeus: A Case Study in Engagement

When Jesus encountered Zacchaeus in Luke 19, He did something unexpected: "Zacchaeus, make haste and come down, for today I must stay at your house."

Jesus invited Himself. Why? Because transformation does not always wait for invitation. Sometimes, it initiates.

And what happened next is critical:

- Zacchaeus welcomed Him
- Zacchaeus gathered his circle
- The environment shifted

And then:

- Repentance occurred
- Restitution was declared
- Generosity was activated

This is powerful: Jesus did not start with correction. He started with a connection. And the connection opened the door for transformation.

That order is deeply important. Jesus was not soft on sin. He was wise about the path that leads a heart toward repentance. He knew that when truth enters through a relationship, it often reaches places that public criticism never can. Zacchaeus was not changed by being shamed from afar. He was changed by being encountered up close.

This also speaks to the believer who wants to represent Christ well. Not every change begins with confrontation. Sometimes it begins with presence, dignity, and an unexpected nearness that leaves a person face-to-face with grace. Grace, when it is real, does not excuse darkness. It exposes it gently enough for repentance to become possible.

Holiness Without Distance

Many believers equate holiness with distance. But Jesus demonstrated something different.

He was:

- Close to sinners
- Yet untouched by sin

Holiness is not isolation from people. Holiness is separation from corruption. This is a major distinction.

Because if holiness requires distance from people, then Jesus Himself would not qualify.

This distinction is necessary in our time. Holiness is often treated as if it were fragile, as though one difficult conversation, one secular environment, or one relationship with a broken person could instantly undo what God has formed. But biblical holiness is not that weak. It is not nervous, brittle, or dependent on perfect surroundings. It is rooted in God, strengthened by conviction, and protected by inward alignment.

Jesus shows us that holiness can remain intact in the presence of disorder. He entered the human mess without becoming part of it. That is not a compromise. That is a strength.

The Fear of Contamination

Let's address a real concern. Some believers avoid engagement because they fear:

- Being influenced
- Being compromised
- Being drawn into the wrong environments

That concern is not entirely wrong. But it reveals something: the issue is not the environment. It is the strength of the believer.

A weak identity fears contamination. A strong identity carries influence.

This is where honest self-examination matters. There are moments when caution is wise, especially if a believer knows his own weaknesses. But there is a difference between healthy discernment and fear-driven retreat. One is led by wisdom. The other is controlled by insecurity. If every difficult environment feels too dangerous to enter, it may be revealing that inward formation still needs to deepen.

The answer is not careless exposure. The answer is deeper strength in God. The believer must become rooted enough in truth, prayer, identity, and spiritual maturity that presence no longer feels like surrender.

Jesus Was Not Influenced; He Influenced

Wherever Jesus went, He did not adapt to the environment. The environment responded to Him.

Sinners did not make Him sinful. His presence made them:

- Reflect
- Repent
- Reconsider their lives

That is influence.

This is the kind of spiritual authority many believers have admired but not fully pursued. Jesus did not enter rooms passively. He carried the presence of the Father into them. His life had substance. His words had weight. His purity had power. Wherever He went, things were forced into decision, hearts softened, hypocrisy surfaced, consciences awakened, and repentance began.

Influence is not merely being present in a room. It is carrying something into that room that the room did not have before you arrived. That is what Jesus did perfectly, and that is what believers are still called to pursue in measure.

"And the light shines in the darkness, and the darkness did not comprehend it." (John 1:5, NKJV)

Light does not negotiate with darkness to be accepted by it. It simply shines, and by shining, it reveals what was hidden.

Religious Criticism vs. Kingdom Reality

Religious minds said, "Why is He with them?" Kingdom reality said, "That is exactly where He should be."

This tension still exists today.

Many believers are more concerned about avoiding association than creating transformation. But Jesus did not protect His reputation at the expense of His mission.

This remains one of the great tests of spiritual maturity. Will we let fear of misunderstanding keep us away from the very people God may be drawing us toward? Will we protect our image more carefully than we pursue our assignment? Jesus never chased the approval of those who mistook distance for righteousness. He remained anchored in the Father's purpose.

Sometimes the believer must be willing to be misunderstood by the overly cautious in order to be faithful to the heart of Christ. That does not mean acting recklessly. It means refusing to let religious discomfort become the ruler of Kingdom obedience.

You cannot Reach People You Refuse to Relate To

Let's make this practical. If believers:

- Only stay among themselves
- Only talk to those who agree
- Only operate in safe environments

Then who reaches:

- The skeptic?
- The atheist?
- The broken?
- The resistant?

The answer becomes obvious: no one.

This is where the cost of distance becomes painfully clear. Whole groups of people remain untouched, not because God is unwilling to reach them, but because many of His people have chosen comfort over contact. We cannot pray for the lost while remaining unwilling to move near them in any meaningful way. At some point, intercession must meet incarnational presence.

This does not mean every believer is called to every environment in the same way. But it does mean no believer should use comfort as a substitute for calling. Someone must be willing to go close enough for love to become believable.

Engagement Is Not Compromise

This must be clearly understood: engagement is not agreement.

Jesus:

- Engaged without endorsing
- Connected without compromising
- Loved without lowering truth

This is the balance the Church must recover.

That balance is precious and necessary. Some believers fear engagement because they assume proximity means approval. But Jesus proves otherwise. He listened without surrendering truth. He loved without blessing sin. He entered broken spaces without adopting broken standards. This is not confusion. It is mature clarity.

The Church does not need less engagement. It needs engagement with deeper conviction, cleaner boundaries, and greater spiritual steadiness. Love becomes most believable when it is neither cold nor compromised.

The Missing Skill: How to Be Present Without Losing Yourself

This is where many struggle. It is not just about being present. It is about:

- Knowing what you carry
- Knowing what you stand on
- Knowing how to respond

Without:

- Blending in
- Backing down
- Becoming silent

This is a skill. And it must be developed.

Many sincere believers fail here, not because they do not love God, but because they have not yet learned how to remain inwardly anchored while outwardly engaged. That kind of steadiness does not happen automatically. It is formed through Scripture, prayer, obedience, reflection, and real-life practice.

To be present without losing yourself, you must know whose you are before you know where you are. You must carry settled convictions before entering unstable environments. You must learn how to listen without absorbing confusion, how to care without being controlled, and how to speak without panic. This is part of spiritual maturity.

From Avoidance to Intentional Presence

The believer must shift from accidental encounters to intentional presence. This means:

- Choosing to be in spaces where light is needed
- Being aware of opportunities to engage
- Recognizing that every interaction is a chance to represent Christ

This shift changes the way ordinary life is seen. The believer stops thinking only in terms of protection and starts thinking in terms of purpose. A workplace, a neighborhood, a meal, a conversation, a moment of tension, a person on the margins, none of these are merely interruptions. They may be invitations.

Intentional presence is not noisy. It is simply awake. It begins to notice where grace may be needed, where truth may be welcomed, where compassion may open a door, and where a faithful response may carry more power than we realize.

The Real Question

The question is no longer, "Should I be around people who believe differently?" The real question is, "Am I strong enough in my identity to be there and still represent Christ accurately?"

That is the deeper question because it turns the focus inward, where growth must happen. The issue is not merely the existence of a difference. The issue is whether the believer has become rooted enough in Christ to stand in the presence of difference without fear, confusion, or compromise. That kind of strength does not come from personality. It comes from formation.

A Call Back to the Model

Jesus did not leave us guessing. He showed us:

- How to enter spaces
- How to engage people
- How to bring transformation

Now the responsibility shifts to us.

Will we continue avoiding, or will we begin engaging?

This chapter leaves us with more than inspiration. It leaves us with a decision. The model of Jesus is clear. The need is still great. The world is still full of people who are broken, skeptical, sinful, wounded, and searching. The question is whether believers will keep protecting themselves from the discomfort of nearness, or whether they will become mature enough to carry the heart of Christ into those very spaces.

Points to Ponder

1. Do I intentionally avoid certain people or environments? Why?
2. Am I more concerned with my comfort or my influence?
3. Do I see engagement as a risk or as an assignment?
4. Am I present enough in the world to actually make an impact?
5. Have I confused holiness with distance in ways that do not reflect the life of Jesus?
6. What kinds of people or settings make me pull back, and what does that reveal about my present level of spiritual strength?
7. Am I willing to let God deepen my convictions so I can remain present without losing clarity?

Call to Action

This week, step intentionally into a space you would normally avoid:

- A conversation
- A relationship
- An environment

Not to blend in, but to:

- Observe
- Connect
- Represent Christ with wisdom and grace

Before you enter that space, pray honestly. Ask the Lord to keep your heart clean, your mind clear, and your spirit sensitive. Do not go in trying to perform or impress. Go in with quiet awareness. Listen carefully. Notice what people carry. Be kind, steady, and truthful. Let your presence reflect Christ before your words try to explain Him.

Declaration

I will not withdraw from the people Jesus came to reach. I am called to engage without compromise. I carry holiness, truth, and grace into every environment. I am not afraid of darkness, because I carry light. My life will reflect the model of Christ. Through me, others will encounter the presence of God.

I do not need distance to remain holy, because my life is anchored in Christ. I will be present where light is needed and clear where truth must be spoken. The love of God in me will not retreat from broken people, and the truth of God in me will not bow to broken systems.

Prayer

Father,

Thank You for the example of Jesus. Forgive me for the times I have avoided people you have called me to reach. Strengthen me to walk in holiness without isolation.

Teach me to engage without compromise. Give me wisdom in conversations, grace in relationships, and boldness in truth. Let my presence bring light wherever I go. Use me to reach those who are far, broken, and searching.

Lord, deliver me from every form of fear that disguises itself as wisdom when it is really avoidance. Deepen my identity in You so that I can be present without becoming unstable. Teach me how to love people sincerely without lowering truth, and how to carry truth clearly without losing tenderness. Let my life reflect the nearness of Christ to those who are wounded, confused, resistant, or ashamed. Make me a believer whose holiness is not fragile, whose convictions are not hidden, and whose presence creates room for grace to work.

In Jesus' name,

Amen.

Chapter 5: Zacchaeus: Salvation That Transforms Systems

When Identity Change Produces Economic and Social Justice

This chapter moves us beyond a narrow view of salvation. It reminds us that when Christ truly enters a life, the change does not remain hidden in private feeling alone. Real salvation reaches values, decisions, habits, resources, and responsibilities. It touches not only what a person believes about eternity, but also how that person lives on earth.

Zacchaeus becomes a striking example of this truth. His story shows us that inward transformation can produce visible correction, generosity, and measurable impact in the world around us.

Most people read the story of Zacchaeus as a simple salvation moment. A sinner meets Jesus. A sinner repents. A sinner is forgiven. And while that is true, it is incomplete. Because what happened in that house was not just a spiritual transformation.

It was a social and economic transformation.

That distinction matters. Too often, salvation is reduced to an inward event with no outward consequence. But the gospel of Jesus Christ was never meant to stop at private comfort. When grace truly enters the heart, it begins to reorder what the heart loves, what the hands do, and what the life produces. Zacchaeus did not merely feel forgiven; he became different.

A Man Embedded in a Corrupt System

Zacchaeus was not just a sinner. He was a systemic participant in injustice. As a chief tax collector:

- He operated within a system that exploited people
- He benefited from overcharging and manipulation
- He represented economic oppression

So when Jesus approached Zacchaeus, He was not just encountering a man. He was confronting a system through a person.

This is one of the most powerful dimensions of the story. Jesus did not begin by attacking the machinery of corruption from a distance. He went directly to the human heart inside it. That is often how the Kingdom works. God reaches systems by transforming the people who sustain them. He exposes injustice, but He also confronts it at its living source, inside motives, decisions, and habits.

Luke 19:2 identifies Zacchaeus plainly: "He was a chief tax collector, and he was rich" (NKJV). His wealth was not presented as a neutral detail. It pointed to a life that had materially benefited from a broken arrangement. That makes the change that follows even more significant.

Jesus entered the System through a relationship

Jesus did not start with:

- A protest
- A public condemnation
- A political statement

He started with: "I must stay at your house."

This is critical. Jesus chose:

- Proximity over distance
- Relationship over rejection

Because transformation rarely happens from the outside. It happens within reach.

These words of Jesus carry great tenderness and great authority at the same time. He did not wait for Zacchaeus to earn nearness. He initiated it. He stepped into the life of a compromised man with deliberate intention. This is the mystery of redemptive love: it comes close enough to confront without first humiliating, and close enough to heal without first pretending sin does not matter.

The believer must not miss this pattern. Jesus did not compromise truth by entering Zacchaeus's house. He positioned truth where it could be fully felt. Presence became the doorway through which conviction could work.

The Power of Presence over Pressure

Many want to change systems through pressure alone. Jesus demonstrates something different:

- Transformation begins with presence
- He did not force Zacchaeus
- He did not shame him publicly
- He created an environment where truth could confront the heart

And when the heart changes, systems begin to shift.

This does not mean pressure is never part of public life, but it does reveal something deeper than pressure can accomplish by itself. External force may restrain behavior for a season, but only inward transformation can produce willing righteousness. Jesus aimed for the center of the man, because once the center changes, everything connected to it becomes vulnerable to God's order.

This is why believers must think carefully about influence. We are often tempted to seek immediate visible change while neglecting the slower, deeper work of the heart. But the Kingdom is not shallow. It transforms people at the root.

The Evidence of True Salvation

Zacchaeus's response was immediate and measurable:

"I give half of my goods to the poor…"

"If I have taken anything from anyone by false accusation, I restore fourfold."

This was not:

- Symbolic
- Emotional
- Temporary

This was:

- Practical

- Financial
- Structural

Let's be clear: salvation that does not affect how a person handles money, power, and people is incomplete.

This is where the story becomes deeply uncomfortable and deeply beautiful. Zacchaeus did not offer vague emotion as proof of change. He offered action. He did not hide behind religious language. He opened his hands. He opened his records. He opened the part of life that most people protect. His repentance became measurable because grace had become real.

Luke 19:8 records his words with striking force: "Look, Lord, I give half of my goods to the poor; and if I have taken anything from anyone by false accusation, I restore fourfold" (NKJV). This was not public theater. It was the fruit of a reordered heart.

From Personal Conversion to Public Impact

What happened in Zacchaeus's house did not stay in his house. Think about it:

- The poor received provisions
- Victims received restitution
- Economic imbalance was corrected

This is social impact, not through policy, but through transformed individuals.

This is where salvation must be understood in its full moral weight. When one person is truly changed by Christ, that change can begin to touch many others. Private repentance can produce public healing. Personal surrender can create communal blessing. What began in one man's heart did not end there; it moved outward into households, relationships, and economic realities.

That pattern still matters today. The Church should never speak of salvation as though it belongs only to inner comfort. Salvation has consequences. It changes how people lead, pay, give, repair, restore, and treat those who have been harmed.

Redistribution as a Result, Not an Agenda

This is where balance is needed. Zacchaeus was not forced to give. He chose to give. This matters because:

- Forced redistribution is external
- Transformed generosity is internal

One is driven by pressure. The other is driven by conviction. And conviction produces sustainability.

This point requires spiritual maturity. The Kingdom does care about the poor, the wronged, and the vulnerable. But the way of Christ begins with a transformed conscience, not empty compulsion. Zacchaeus gave because the truth had reached him. His generosity was not extracted. It was awakened. And what is awakened by grace often carries a freedom and durability that external force alone cannot create.

This does not weaken the seriousness of justice; it deepens it. God desires more than visible compliance. He desires a heart that has come into agreement with what is right.

The Kingdom Approach to Social Ethics

The Kingdom does not ignore social issues, but it approaches them differently.

The world says: Change systems to change people. The Kingdom says: Change people, and they will transform systems.

Zacchaeus proves this. One transformed man:

- Released resources
- Corrected injustice
- Impacted a community

This is not simplistic thinking. Systems do matter. Structures do matter. Justice matters. But the Kingdom refuses to separate these realities from the human heart. Scripture consistently shows that when people remain inwardly corrupt, even good structures can be manipulated. Yet when hearts are brought under the lordship of Christ, those same people can become agents of repair, righteousness, and tangible mercy.

Ezekiel 36:26 captures the spirit of this pattern: "I will give you a new heart and put a new spirit within you" (NKJV). God's answer to brokenness is not only regulation from the outside, but renewal from within.

Why This Matters Today

Many believers struggle with:

- Economic injustice
- Poverty
- Social imbalance

And the responses often fall into extremes:

- Ignore the problem
- Or adopt purely political solutions

But the story of Zacchaeus invites a Kingdom response that is deeper than denial and more transformative than slogans. It calls believers to ask hard questions about integrity, responsibility, restoration, and the use of influence. It challenges us not merely to discuss brokenness, but to let God examine where our own lives may be participating in, benefiting from, or ignoring what is unjust.

The modern believer must not become passive in the face of suffering, nor careless in the face of complexity. We are called to bring a distinctly Christ-centered response, one that values truth, repentance, generosity, justice, and inward transformation together.

Transformation through Identity-Driven Action

This phrase captures the heart of the chapter. Zacchaeus did not change because he was merely instructed. He changed because his encounter with Jesus touched identity, allegiance, and value. Once that happened, action followed. What a person believes he is before

God will eventually shape what that person does with power, money, and opportunity.

You cannot Preach Salvation without Expecting Change.

Let's be honest. If salvation:

- Does not change values
- Does not affect decisions
- Does not influence behavior

Then what exactly has been saved?

Zacchaeus did not need:

- A financial seminar
- A policy reform

He needed an encounter. And that encounter reordered everything.

This is a needed challenge in every generation. We must not reduce salvation to verbal agreement while leaving conduct untouched. The grace that saves also teaches, corrects, softens, and redirects. It does not leave a person permanently at peace with the very patterns from which Christ came to deliver him.

Titus 2:11–12 says, "For the grace of God that brings salvation has appeared to all men, teaching us that, denying ungodliness and worldly lusts, we should live soberly, righteously, and godly in the present age" (NKJV). Grace is not passive permission. Grace is holy instruction.

Jesus Addressed More Than Sin, He Addressed Impact

When Jesus said, "Today salvation has come to this house…" He was not only acknowledging forgiveness. He was recognizing:

- Restoration
- Alignment
- Transformation with visible impact

Salvation touched:

- His identity
- His relationships
- His finances

This is holistic.

That sentence from Jesus is full of wonder. Salvation came to the house, not merely to a private inner feeling. The whole atmosphere changed. The direction of the household changed. The social consequences of one man's repentance began to emerge. This is the breadth of God's redeeming work. He touches the soul, but He also begins to touch the life built around that soul.

Luke 19:9 declares, "Today salvation has come to this house" (NKJV). Jesus saw more than emotion. He saw evidence that grace had already begun to rearrange reality.

The Missing Link in Modern Christianity

Many believers accept salvation but disconnect it from responsibility. They think, "I am saved," yet continue in:

- Unjust practices
- Self-centered living
- Indifference to others

Zacchaeus shows us that true salvation produces accountability and generosity.

This is where the chapter presses on the conscience. Salvation is not a license to remain unchanged while speaking the language of faith. It is an invitation into a life that can no longer remain at peace with selfishness, dishonesty, and indifference. The believer who has truly met Christ cannot keep treating people, possessions, and privilege exactly the same way.

From Blessing to Responsibility

When identity is restored:

- Wealth is no longer for accumulation alone
- Power is no longer for control
- Influence is no longer for self

Everything becomes a tool for:

- Restoration
- Justice
- Impact

That is one of the most beautiful shifts in Christian maturity. A person begins to stop asking only, "What can I gain?" and starts asking, "What can God do through what has been placed in my hands?" Blessing becomes stewardship. Possession becomes responsibility. Influence becomes service.

This is not a loss. It is alignment. It is the liberation of purpose. A life under Christ no longer treats resources as private trophies, but as entrusted instruments that can reflect the heart of God.

What Would Happen If This Were Normal?

Imagine a Church where:

- Business owners operated with integrity
- Leaders corrected past wrongs
- Believers used resources to lift others

You would not need:

- External pressure
- Constant regulation

Because transformation would flow from within.

This vision is not unrealistic in the Kingdom. It is exactly the kind of witness that makes the gospel visible. When believers become known for honesty, repair, generosity, fairness, and practical mercy, Christianity stops sounding abstract. It begins to take on flesh in the eyes of others. Communities feel it. Families benefit from it. Systems are affected by it.

The Call to Economic Integrity

Zacchaeus forces us to ask:

- How do I handle money?
- Have I wronged anyone?
- Am I using my resources for impact?

This is where Christianity becomes visible, not just in what we say, but in what we do.

These are not comfortable questions, but they are holy ones. They invite the believer to move beyond admiration of the story and into honest self-examination. We are not all tax collectors, but every believer still faces the issue of stewardship, fairness, responsibility, and the moral use of influence.

A Pattern for Kingdom Influence

Let's summarize the pattern:

- **Engagement**, Jesus enters the space
- **Connection**, Relationship is established
- **Transformation**, Identity is restored
- **Action**, Behavior changes
- **Impact**, Society is affected

This is Kingdom social ethics.

This pattern is worth lingering over because it reveals how God often works in the world. He enters what is broken, not to leave it untouched, but to redeem it from the inside out. The Church must learn this rhythm well. We are not sent merely to make statements. We are sent to carry the presence and truth of Christ in ways that can awaken transformation.

A Challenge to the Believer

The question is no longer, "Am I saved?" The question is, "Is my salvation producing visible transformation around me?"

Because if it is not, something is missing.

That is not a call to perform for appearance. It is a call to let grace have its full way. The issue is not whether every life looks dramatic in the same manner. The issue is whether salvation is bearing fruit, fruit in character, fruit in integrity, fruit in justice, fruit in generosity, fruit in how others are affected by our obedience.

Points to Ponder

1. Has my salvation affected how I handle money and resources?
2. Am I aware of any areas where I need to make things right?
3. Do I see my influence as a tool for impact or for personal gain?
4. Is my faith producing visible change beyond my personal life?
5. Have I allowed grace to reach the practical parts of my life, or have I kept faith mostly in the realm of words and private belief?
6. Is there any area where the Holy Spirit is inviting me to move from regret into restitution, from possession into generosity, or from comfort into responsibility?

Call to Action

Take time this week to evaluate:

- Your finances
- Your relationships
- Your areas of influence

Ask: "Where can I bring restoration, generosity, or justice?" Then act on one specific area.

Do not let the response remain theoretical. Choose one clear step. It may be correcting a wrong, repaying a debt, helping someone in need, changing an unjust practice, becoming more transparent, or using your resources in a more God-honoring way. Let obedience become visible.

Declaration

My salvation is real and active. It transforms how I live, give, and lead. I walk in integrity, justice, and generosity. What God has placed in my hands will be used for impact. Through me, lives will be restored, and communities will be changed.

I will not separate my faith from my stewardship, my influence, or my responsibility. The grace of God in my life is producing fruit that can be seen, felt, and trusted. What Christ has changed in me will begin to bless others around me.

Prayer

Father,

Thank You for the transformation You have begun in me. Help me to live out my salvation in practical ways. Show me where I need to make things right. Give me the courage to act with integrity and generosity.

Teach me to use what I have for Your purposes. Let my life reflect not only belief, but impact.

Lord, examine every hidden place where selfishness, fear, or convenience has kept me from obeying You fully. Show me where I have separated spirituality from stewardship, confession from correction, or blessing from responsibility. Give me a clean heart and honest hands. Teach me to handle money, influence, and opportunity in a way that honors You and serves people well. Where restitution is needed, give me courage. Where generosity is needed, give me the willingness. Where justice is needed, give me discernment. Let my salvation become visible in the way I live, and let the fruit of that obedience bring healing, relief, and hope to others.

In Jesus' name,

Amen.

Chapter 6: The Failure Of Withdrawn Faith

Why Avoidance Has Become One of the Church's Greatest Weaknesses

There is a kind of faith that appears clean on the outside but quietly fails its assignment in the world. It avoids tension, keeps a safe distance, and mistakes separation for strength. Yet when we look closely at the life of Jesus, we find something very different. He was holy, but never absent. He was separate from sin, but never detached from people.

This chapter confronts the weakness of withdrawn faith and calls the believer back to a faith that is present, courageous, and useful in the places where truth is most needed.

There is a dangerous pattern in modern Christianity. It is the pattern of withdrawal. Not necessarily withdrawal from the church. Not withdrawal from belief. Not withdrawal from spiritual language. But withdrawal from meaningful engagement with the world.

Many believers are still:

- Attending services
- Singing songs
- Using Christian vocabulary

But in practice, they have withdrawn from:

- Cultural conversations
- Difficult environments
- Relationships with people outside their comfort zone

And this withdrawal is often treated as wisdom. But it is not wisdom. It is a failure.

That word may sound strong, but it is necessary. When the Church retreats from the very places where truth, love, and clarity are needed, something essential is lost. A faith that remains active only within protected circles may feel sincere, but it cannot fully reflect the mission of Christ. Withdrawal may protect comfort, but it rarely fulfills calling.

Faith Was Never Meant to Be Private Protection Only

Faith is personal. But it was never meant to remain private in function. Jesus did not save us merely so we could:

- Feel secure
- Stay encouraged
- Remain spiritually comforted

He saved us to:

- Represent Him
- Carry truth
- Reveal light

And representation requires presence.

This is where many believers unintentionally shrink the meaning of faith. They receive comfort from God, but do not move with God. They cherish personal devotion, but do not always allow that devotion to become visible obedience in the world around them. Yet biblical faith does not end in private reassurance. It moves outward in witness, character, courage, and presence.

"You are the light of the world. A city that is set on a hill cannot be hidden" (Matthew 5:14, NKJV). Jesus did not describe believers as hidden comfort for themselves. He described them as visible light for others.

The Problem with Withdrawn Faith

Withdrawn faith looks safe. It looks disciplined. It looks cautious. It even looks holy. But underneath, it often reveals:

- Fear of discomfort
- Fear of opposition
- Fear of contamination
- Fear of being challenged

So instead of engaging the world with prepared conviction, many believers build lives that minimize contact with it. Over time, this creates a Christianity that is:

- Sheltered
- Reactionary
- Ineffective

The tragedy is that sheltered faith often believes it is being faithful while slowly becoming unprepared. The less it engages, the less it understands. The less it understands, the more threatening the world appears. And the more threatening the world appears, the more it withdraws. In this way, fear can quietly become a cycle disguised as maturity.

This is why avoidance must be named honestly. Not all distance is discernment. Sometimes it is spiritual hesitation that has been given respectable language.

Salt That Never Touches Anything

Jesus called His followers the salt of the earth. Salt only works through contact. If salt never touches what it was meant to preserve, its nature may remain intact, but its purpose is wasted.

This is the failure of withdrawn faith. It keeps its form, but loses its function.

That image should sober us. Salt does not fulfill its assignment by admiring its own purity from a distance. Its usefulness is proven in contact. In the same way, Christian conviction cannot remain meaningful if it never enters real situations, real relationships, real pressures, and real human needs.

A believer may preserve personal morality and still fail to preserve anything around him if he remains absent from the places where God intended his witness to matter.

Why the Church Retreats

Let us be honest about the reasons. The Church often withdraws because engagement is costly. Engagement means:

- Listening to painful stories
- Answering difficult questions
- Facing intellectual pressure
- Encountering moral brokenness
- Standing firm in uncomfortable spaces

That is harder than staying inside familiar circles. So many choose comfort over calling.

This choice is rarely announced openly. It happens quietly, little by little. A believer stops entering certain conversations, stops building certain relationships, and stops showing up in difficult spaces. Eventually, faith becomes highly active in safe environments and strangely absent in the places where witness would require courage.

Comfort is understandable, but it cannot become our ruler. The gospel has never called us to the easiest path of self-protection. It calls us to faithful presence.

Jesus Did Not Withdraw

If anyone had reason to remain separate, it was Jesus. Yet He moved toward:

- The broken
- The skeptical

- The sinful
- The rejected

He did not fear proximity. He did not hide from tension. He did not avoid difficult people. He remained pure, but He remained present. This is the pattern.

Jesus did not float above human struggle as though holiness required emotional or relational distance. He entered homes, streets, questions, grief, tension, and contradiction. He allowed Himself to be interrupted by need and surrounded by people who were confused, sinful, proud, hurting, or desperate. Still, He never lost himself.

This is why His example remains so confronting. It removes our excuses while also revealing our calling. He shows us that holiness and mission were never meant to oppose each other.

Withdrawal Creates Misrepresentation

When believers withdraw, the world learns the wrong lesson. It begins to assume:

- Christians do not understand real life
- Christians cannot handle questions
- Christians only function in safe spaces

And sadly, in many cases, that assumption is reinforced by behavior.

This is not merely a public relations problem. It is a witness problem. The issue is not whether believers are liked by the world, but whether Christ is being represented truthfully through them. If our faith cannot remain present in places of tension, people may conclude that Christianity offers comfort without substance, conviction without courage, or morality without compassion.

That is not the Jesus of Scripture. And it must not become the image people learn from us.

The Cost of Absence

When believers are absent from the world's harder spaces:

- Broken voices go unheard
- Confused minds go unanswered
- Wounded people go unreached

The Church then complains about darkness while refusing to stand where light is needed.

That is a contradiction.

We cannot meaningfully lament decline while retreating from responsibility. We cannot pray for transformation and then remain unwilling to enter the places where transformation may begin through faithful presence. The absence of believers in difficult spaces leaves a vacuum, and vacuums never remain empty for long. Other voices fill them. Other values shape them. Other influences take root.

The cost of absence is often paid by the very people Christ would have us love.

Faith Must Be Strong Enough to Remain Present

The answer is not careless exposure. The answer is a stronger formation. Believers must become spiritually mature enough to:

- Enter hard spaces
- Remain clear
- Stay uncompromised
- Speak truth with grace

This requires more than sincerity. It requires depth.

This is an important distinction. The solution to withdrawn faith is not reckless involvement or shallow activism. It is inward strength. The believer must be formed deeply enough in Christ that he no longer sees every difficult environment as a threat to survival. Instead, he learns to stand there as a witness.

"Be watchful, stand fast in the faith, be brave, be strong" (1 Corinthians 16:13, NKJV). Scripture does not call believers to nervous retreat. It calls them to alert, grounded courage.

Withdrawal Is Often a Sign of Unfinished Identity

At its deepest level, withdrawn faith usually reveals identity weakness. If I am unsure of who I am in Christ, then every opposing space feels larger than me. But when identity is settled:

- I can enter without panic
- I can listen without collapsing
- I can speak without fear

So the problem is not only external. It is internal.

This is why true renewal cannot begin only with strategy. It must also involve identity. The believer who knows he belongs to God, who knows Christ is enough, and who knows truth is not fragile will engage differently. He may still feel the weight of difficult spaces, but he will no longer be ruled by them.

Identity steadies presence. It gives the soul a place to stand before it ever enters the room.

The Difference between Separation and Withdrawal

Biblical separation means:

- Being distinct in values
- Being holy in conduct
- Being governed by truth

But withdrawal means:

- Being absent from the assignment
- Being silent in responsibility
- Being disconnected from people who need light

These are not the same thing. And the Church must stop confusing them.

This confusion has done quite a damage for generations. Some believers have treated distance itself as proof of faithfulness, when in reality the deeper question is whether Christ is being represented where He has sent us. Biblical separation is inward allegiance that shapes outward conduct. Withdrawal is often the refusal to remain available where the mission becomes inconvenient.

One honors God. The other often protects oneself.

The Fear behind the Distance

Why do many believers stay away? Because distance feels easier than tension. Distance protects the image. Distance avoids conflict. Distance reduces risk. But distance also reduces influence.

This is the trade many do not realize they are making. The more we arrange our lives to avoid discomfort, the less useful we become in the places where truth must be carried with patience and courage. Safety has a place, but when safety becomes the ruling value, the mission begins to weaken.

A faith that cannot bear tension will rarely produce transformation.

What the World Needs from Believers

The world does not need believers who disappear. It needs believers who can:

- Remain present without compromise
- Speak clearly without arrogance
- Love deeply without surrendering truth

This is rare. And that is exactly why it matters.

People do not need a Church that only knows how to preach from a distance. They need to encounter believers whose lives hold conviction and compassion together. They need to see that truth can be carried by people who are not panicked, harsh, or evasive.

This kind of presence becomes a testimony in itself. It tells the world that Christ forms people who can stand with both grace and strength.

A Church That Engages Looks More Like Jesus

A healthy Church is not one that merely protects itself. It is one that:

- Understands the times
- Knows the truth
- Enters the world intentionally
- Carries Christ into real places

That is the Church Jesus envisioned.

The beauty of such a Church is that it does not lose holiness by becoming present. It reveals holiness more fully. It becomes a living witness that the gospel can survive scrutiny, endure pain, answer confusion, and remain pure while doing so.

This is the kind of Christianity that can disciple generations, strengthen communities, and reflect the heart of Jesus more accurately.

From Sheltered Faith to Send Faith

The believer must move from:

- Sheltered faith
  to
- Sent faith

From:

- Avoiding hard places
  to
- Entering them with wisdom

From:

- Preserving comfort
  to
- Fulfilling assignment

Sent faith understands that every ordinary space may become a place of witness. It does not wait for perfect conditions. It learns to walk prayerfully, think clearly, and remain available to God in real life. This kind of faith does not glorify danger, but neither does it worship comfort.

It remembers that we were not merely saved from something. We were also sent into something.

A Necessary Conviction

This chapter is not asking whether believers still have faith. It is asking whether their faith is functioning because faith that never enters real life cannot fully reflect the Christ who entered ours.

That is the question that must stay with us. Not simply, "Do I believe?" but "Where is my belief visible in mission, presence, courage, and usefulness?" The goal is not guilt. The goal is awakening.

Points to Ponder

1. Have I withdrawn from spaces where my faith should be present?
2. Do I confuse distance with holiness?
3. What kinds of environments make me retreat, and why?
4. Is my faith functioning in the real world, or only in safe settings?
5. Have I built a version of Christianity that protects me more than it prepares me?
6. Where has comfort replaced calling in my daily life?
7. What would it look like for my faith to become more present, more useful, and more visible in the world around me?

Call to Action

This week, identify one area where you have been spiritually absent:

- A relationship
- A conversation
- A setting
- A responsibility

Then prayerfully re-enter it with wisdom and intention.

Do not rush in with noise or pressure. Go back in with humility, prayer, and a clear purpose. Ask God to show you how to be present in a way that reflects Christ well. Let this be a step away from passive withdrawal and toward faithful witness.

Declaration

My faith will not hide. My faith will function. I am called to be present, clear, and useful. I do not withdraw from the world God has sent me to reach. I carry light into real places and truth into real conversations. Through Christ, I will remain strong, holy, and engaged.

I reject every pattern of fearful withdrawal that has kept my witness small. I am not called merely to stay safe; I am called to stay faithful. My life will reflect a faith that is present enough to serve and strong enough to stand.

Prayer

Father,

Forgive me for every way I have withdrawn from places where You called me to be present. Forgive me for choosing comfort when You were calling me to courage. Strengthen my faith so that it functions in real life. Teach me to remain holy without becoming absent. Teach me to remain present without becoming compromised.

Give me wisdom, stability, and love. Let my life reflect Jesus in the spaces where light is most needed.

Lord, break every pattern in me that has mistaken avoidance for faithfulness. Heal the fear that has made me step back from difficult people, difficult questions, and difficult places. Deepen my identity in You until my heart is no longer ruled by the need for safety, approval, or ease. Make me strong enough to remain present, clear enough to speak when needed, and tender enough to love people well in the middle of brokenness. Let my faith become active, visible, and useful in the world around me. May I not only believe in private, but represent You faithfully in public.

In Jesus' name,

Amen.

Chapter 7: "Come Out From Among Them"

Separation Without Isolation:

Understanding What God Actually Meant

Some verses become anchors in the believer's life. Others become walls when they are misunderstood. This chapter helps us slow down and read carefully, because spiritual language can sometimes be used to support fear instead of truth. God does call His people to be separate, but He does not call them to become absent, unreachable, or disconnected from the very people they were sent to love.

To understand this rightly is to recover both holiness and mission at the same time.

There are scriptures that guide us. And there are scriptures that, when misunderstood, limit us. This is one of them: "Come out from among them and be separate, says the Lord...", 2 Corinthians 6:17.

For many believers, this verse has become a justification for:

- Withdrawal
- Isolation
- Disengagement from the world

But when interpreted incorrectly, it creates a version of Christianity that Jesus Himself did not model.

This is why careful interpretation matters. A verse can be true, holy, and necessary, yet still be misapplied in ways that weaken the believer's witness. When separation is interpreted as total distance from people, society, or difficult environments, it can quietly train Christians to retreat where they should remain present. The result is not greater holiness, but reduced usefulness.

The Misinterpretation That Created Distance

Many have understood this scripture to mean:

- Avoid unbelievers
- Separate from society
- Stay within "safe" Christian environments

But if this were true, then Jesus:

- Would not eat with sinners
- Would not enter their homes
- Would not engage their world

And yet, He did all of these.

So we must ask: what does "separation" really mean?

That question is essential. It forces us to look beyond tradition, assumptions, and inherited habits. If our interpretation leads us away from the very pattern Jesus lived, then something in our understanding must be corrected. Scripture does not contradict Christ. It must be read through the wisdom, character, and example of Christ.

Context Matters

Paul is not telling believers to avoid people. He is addressing partnership with unrighteousness.

Let's look at the broader context:

"What fellowship has righteousness with lawlessness?" "What communion has light with darkness?" 2 Corinthians 6:14

The issue is not presence. The issue is participation.

This is the turning point of the passage. Paul is not warning believers against proximity to unbelievers; he is warning them against spiritual compromise and binding alignment with what opposes God. There is a real difference between being present in a broken world and becoming joined to its broken patterns. One is a mission. The other is compromise. Confusing those two has created unnecessary fear in many believers.

The believer must learn to see this distinction clearly. Presence says, "I am here to represent Christ." Participation says, "I am now sharing in what opposes Him." Scripture forbids the second, not the first.

Separation Is About Identity, Not Distance

This is the key: separation is not physical. It is spiritual and ethical.

It means:

- Do not adopt the values of darkness
- Do not participate in unrighteous practices
- Do not compromise your convictions

But it does not mean:

- Remove yourself from people
- Avoid engagement
- Live disconnected from society

Separation, in its healthiest biblical sense, is about inner allegiance. It is about who shapes you, what governs you, what defines your values, and what your life ultimately reflects. A believer can stand in a secular office, a difficult classroom, a tense conversation, or a morally confused society and still remain separate in spirit, conviction, and conduct.

This is why separation cannot be measured merely by distance. A person may be physically removed from many things and still be inwardly compromised. Another may be fully present in difficult environments and yet remain deeply governed by God. The deeper issue is always formation, not location.

Jesus: The Perfect Balance

Jesus was:

- Fully present
- Fully engaged
- Fully accessible

And yet:

- Fully holy
- Fully uncompromised
- Fully aligned with the Father

He proves something powerful: you can be surrounded by darkness without being shaped by it.

This balance is one of the most beautiful things about the life of Jesus. He did not panic in the presence of sin, nor did He blend into it. He remained so rooted in the Father that no environment had the power to redefine Him. His holiness was not fragile. His identity was not negotiable. His mission was not interrupted by the discomfort of being near broken people.

That is the pattern the Church must recover. Not fearful isolation. Not careless blending in. But steady, holy presence.

Hebrews 7:26 describes Jesus as "holy, harmless, undefiled, separate from sinners" (NKJV). Yet in the Gospels, He is constantly among sinners. This shows us that biblical separation is not distance from people, but freedom from their corruption.

The Danger of Misapplied Separation

When separation is misunderstood, it produces:

- Isolation instead of influence
- Fear instead of confidence
- Silence instead of engagement

And over time, the Church becomes:

- Irrelevant to society
- Absent from key spaces
- Unable to shape culture

Not because it lacks truth, but because it has removed itself from where truth is needed.

This is one of the quiet tragedies of modern Christianity. Believers may preserve language, routines, and religious habits, yet still lose the courage to remain present where Christ is needed most. Misapplied separation produces a smaller witness, a thinner voice, and a weaker public faith. It can make believers feel safe while leaving whole environments untouched by truth.

The issue is not that the Church has nothing to offer. The issue is that too often it is not close enough to offer it.

Salt That Never Leaves the Shaker

Jesus also said: "You are the salt of the earth…", Matthew 5:13

Salt has a purpose:

- To preserve
- To influence
- To bring change

But salt only works when it is:

- Applied
- Spread
- Present

Salt that stays in the container is useless.

In the same way, a believer who never engages cannot influence.

This image is simple but deeply searching. Salt can remain perfectly salt while doing absolutely nothing if it never leaves the shaker. In the same way, a believer may keep sound doctrine, right convictions, and moral boundaries, yet still fail in mission if none of it ever reaches the places where decay is spreading.

Christian maturity is not measured only by what we avoid. It is also measured by whether our lives are useful in the hands of God.

The Fear behind Isolation

Let's be honest again. Some separation is not spiritual. It is fear. Fear of:

- Being challenged
- Being rejected
- Being exposed
- Being influenced

This honesty matters because fear often dresses itself in religious language. What looks like holiness on the outside may sometimes be self-protection underneath. A believer may say he is being cautious, but in truth, he may simply be uncomfortable with tension, disagreement, or vulnerability. Until this is faced honestly, growth remains limited.

Of course, believers should be discerning. Not every environment is wise in every season. Not every relationship has healthy boundaries. But discernment and fear are not the same thing. Discernment is led by truth. Fear is led by self-protection.

A Weak Identity Uses Separation as a Shield

When identity is unclear, distance feels safer, because distance protects you from:

- Questions you cannot answer
- Environments you cannot navigate
- People who may challenge what you believe

So instead of growing stronger, many simply pull further away. But this is not maturity. It is avoidance.

This is why identity remains central to the whole message of your manuscript. A believer who knows who he is in Christ does not need separation as a shield against every uncomfortable space. He can remain present because his center is not being built by the environment around him. He already stands on something deeper.

Weak identity often seeks safety by reducing exposure. Strong identity seeks faithfulness by increasing readiness. One retreats because it feels threatened. The other engages because it knows what it carries.

Separation Should Strengthen Engagement, Not Prevent It

Biblical separation should make a believer:

- Clearer
- Stronger
- More grounded

Not:

- More distant
- More fearful
- More passive

In other words, you are separated from darkness so that you can shine in it more effectively.

This is the proper purpose of holiness. God sets His people apart so that their lives become more useful, not less. He forms conviction in us so we can stand in confusing places without losing ourselves. He strengthens purity in us so we can enter broken spaces without agreeing with them. Separation is not an exit from the mission. It is preparation for the mission.

"That you may become blameless and harmless, children of God without fault in the midst of a crooked and perverse generation, among whom you shine as lights in the world" (Philippians 2:15, NKJV)

Notice the language: in the midst of, not far away from.

The Difference between Contact and Contamination

Many believers fear that contact automatically leads to contamination. But this is not always true. Jesus had contact without contamination. The apostles had contact without contamination. The early Church had contact without contamination.

The real question is not, "Am I around darkness?" The real question is, "Am I rooted enough not to absorb it?"

This is where spiritual formation becomes essential. The answer to contamination is not total distance from society, but deeper rootedness in Christ. A believer who is prayerless, ungrounded, and inwardly unstable may indeed struggle in certain environments. But the solution is not to glorify retreat. The solution is to grow stronger in truth, prayer, discernment, and identity.

The more rooted we become, the less easily we are moved. The more deeply we are formed by God, the more clearly we can remain present without becoming confused.

The Church Must Teach Both Holiness and Presence

Some churches emphasize holiness but forget presence. Others emphasize presence but neglect holiness. But Jesus held both together.

The Church must do the same. Because without holiness, engagement becomes compromise. And without presence, holiness becomes absence.

This balance is not optional. It is part of mature discipleship. A church that teaches holiness without presence may raise believers who stay clean but remain ineffective. A church that teaches presence without holiness may raise believers who are active but unanchored. Neither reflects the fullness of Christ.

What is needed now is a generation of believers who can carry conviction without withdrawal and compassion without compromise.

A Practical Picture of Separation

What does healthy separation look like?

It means:

- Being in conversations without adopting ungodly values
- Working in environments without losing integrity
- Loving people without approving sin
- Being present in society without being shaped by its rebellion

That is biblical separation.

This is practical holiness. It is not dramatic, distant, or performative. It is steady. It is visible in choices, speech, priorities, boundaries, and posture. It is a believer who can stay in the room and still remain inwardly governed by Christ.

This kind of life becomes a quiet testimony. People begin to see someone who is close enough to care, yet strong enough not to drift.

A Needed Correction

The command to "come out" was never meant to create a Church that hides. It was meant to create a Church that remains distinct.

Distinct in:

- Character
- Conviction
- Conduct

But still present enough to be useful.

That distinction matters greatly. God does not call His people out so they can disappear. He calls them out so they can belong to Him clearly, live differently, and reflect His nature in the world. Separation is about ownership before it is about movement. It is the mark of a people who know whose they are.

A Call to Mature Presence

The goal is not to become less holy. The goal is to become holy enough to remain present, holy enough to:

- Stand in difficult spaces
- Love difficult people
- Carry truth into confusing environments

without losing your identity.

This is a mature presence. It is not the loud confidence of performance. It is the calm steadiness of a believer who has been formed by God enough to stay available to God. It knows how to remain in the world without borrowing the world's spirit.

That kind of presence is powerful. It does not always announce itself, but it leaves a mark.

Points to Ponder

1. Have I used "separation" as a reason to avoid engagement?
2. Am I avoiding people, or avoiding compromise?
3. Is my identity strong enough to sustain presence in challenging environments?
4. Where might God be calling me to engage instead of withdraw?
5. Have I confused fear-based distance with biblical holiness?
6. What situations reveal whether I am truly rooted in Christ or merely protected by comfort?
7. In what area is God inviting me to become more spiritually mature so I can remain present without losing clarity?

Call to Action

Identify one area where you have withdrawn out of fear. Re-engage intentionally this week:

- With clarity
- With conviction
- With wisdom

Not to blend in, but to stand out.

Before you re-enter that space, spend time with God and ask Him to search your motives. Let Him show you whether your distance has been rooted in wisdom or avoidance. Then go back prayerfully, not casually. Remain kind, clear, and grounded. Let your presence become an expression of obedience, not just effort.

Declaration

I am set apart, but not set aside. I walk in holiness without isolation. I am present in the world, but not shaped by it. My identity is secure, and my convictions are firm. I will engage with wisdom, clarity, and boldness. Through me, God's light will shine in every environment.

I do not confuse separation with retreat, because God has called me to be distinct and useful. I will remain rooted in Christ, steady in truth, and available for His purpose wherever He sends me. The holiness of God in me will not make me disappear from the world; it will make me shine within it.

Prayer

Father,

Thank you for calling me to be set apart. Help me to understand what that truly means. Remove every fear that causes me to withdraw unnecessarily. Strengthen me to walk in holiness while remaining engaged. Teach me to stand firm in my identity, no matter the environment. Let my life reflect both purity and presence. Use me as a light in places where darkness exists.

Lord, correct every misunderstanding in me that has made distance feel safer than obedience. Teach me to love holiness without using it as a hiding place. Strengthen my inner life so deeply that I can remain present in difficult spaces without absorbing what is not from You. Let my convictions be clear, my heart be clean, and my witness be strong. Make me a believer who is distinct without becoming detached, faithful without becoming fearful, and present without becoming compromised. Let my life reflect the beauty of a holiness that still knows how to reach people.

In Jesus' name,

Amen.

Chapter 8: In The World, Not Of It

Why Jesus Prayed for Our Presence, Not Our Escape

This chapter touches on one of the most important tensions in the believer's life. Many Christians sincerely want to remain pure, protected, and faithful, yet they quietly assume that distance from the world is the safest way to do that. But when Jesus prayed for His followers, He revealed something deeper. He did not ask the Father to remove us from the world. He asked that we would remain in it under divine protection, divine truth, and divine purpose.

That changes how we see our surroundings, our struggles, and our assignment.

There is no clearer statement about the believer's relationship with the world than the prayer of Jesus in John 17. This is not a sermon. This is not a parable. This is Jesus speaking directly to the Father, revealing His deepest intention for those who would follow Him. And what He prays may surprise many.

What makes this prayer so powerful is that it opens the heart of Christ in a very personal way. We are not merely hearing instruction here; we are hearing intercession. We are listening to what Jesus desired for His people while speaking to the Father Himself. That gives this passage unusual weight. It is not speculation. It is not a theory. It is the revealed desire of the Son concerning those who belong to Him.

Jesus Did Not Pray for Removal

Let's begin with what Jesus did not ask: "I do not pray that You should take them out of the world…", John 17:15

This settles the matter immediately.

Jesus did not ask for:

- Escape
- Separation by distance
- Removal from difficult environments

In fact, He explicitly rejected that idea.

Why? Because removal cancels the assignment.

This truth corrects a great deal of hidden fear in the believer. If Jesus Himself did not ask for our escape, then we must stop imagining that safety is found only in distance. He understood the pressures we would face, the darkness we would encounter, and the challenges of remaining faithful in a broken world. Yet even knowing all of that, He still prayed for our presence, not our disappearance.

The World Is Not the Problem, It Is the Assignment

Many believers see the world as:

- A threat
- A distraction
- A place to endure until heaven

But Jesus sees the world differently. He sees it as:

- A field
- A mission
- A place of impact

If the world were only a danger, Jesus would have asked for our removal. Instead, He prays for something else.

This is a needed change in perspective. The world is not merely the backdrop of our waiting. It is the setting of our witness. It is where truth must be carried, where light must be seen, where grace must be embodied, and where the life of Christ in us must become visible. A believer who only sees the world as danger will spend most of their life trying to avoid it. A believer who sees the world as an assignment will begin to ask how God wants to use him within it.

Jesus said elsewhere, "Lift up your eyes and look at the fields, for they are already white for harvest!" (John 4:35, NKJV) That is not the language of retreat. It is the language of mission.

Protection without Isolation

Jesus continues: "…but that You should keep them from the evil one."

Notice the balance:

- Not removed from the world
- But protected within it

This is powerful.

God's strategy is not distance. It is protection plus presence.

This balance is beautiful because it removes two extremes at once. It removes the fear that says we must run from the world to survive, and it also removes the carelessness that says presence needs no protection. Jesus asks neither for escape nor for unguarded exposure. He asks for divine keeping. That means the believer is not left alone in difficult environments. God's presence is not absent from the places where He sends us.

There is deep comfort in this. We are not preserved by isolation alone. We are preserved by the faithfulness of God. He is able to keep what He sends. He is able to guard the heart, steady the mind, strengthen conviction, and protect the inner life of the believer who remains surrendered to Him.

Identity Within Environment

Jesus then says: "They are not of the world, just as I am not of the world.", John 17:16

This is the distinction.

You are:

- In the world
- But not of it

Meaning: you operate in it, but you are not defined by it. This is identity language.

These words are deeply stabilizing because they remind us that location does not determine identity. You may live in a confused generation, work in a secular system, or move through environments that do not honor God, yet none of those things have the authority to define who you are. The believer's identity is not built by the surrounding culture. It is rooted in Christ.

That is why remaining present does not have to become spiritual confusion. You can be fully present in a place without allowing that place to become your source. Your values, your convictions, your inner formation, and your direction all come from something higher.

Sent, Not Stranded

Then Jesus makes it even clearer: "As You sent Me into the world, I also have sent them into the world.", John 17:18

This changes everything.

You are not:

- Accidentally in the world
- Stuck in a difficult environment

You are sent. And if you are sent, then:

- Your environment is not random
- Your interactions are not meaningless
- Your presence carries purpose

The word sent is full of dignity. It means the believer is not wandering through life without meaning. It means even ordinary places can carry holy significance. The workplace, the school, the neighborhood, the family space, the difficult room, the public setting, the private conversation, none of these are necessarily random when seen through the eyes of Christ. The believer is there as one commissioned.

This is why spiritual passivity must give way to awareness. If I know I am sent, then I can no longer treat my life as accidental. I begin to ask different questions. Not, "Why am I forced to be here?" but, "Lord, why did You send me here, and how do You want to be represented through me?"

Jesus' Model Becomes Our Mandate

Jesus says: "As You sent Me…"

Meaning: the same way Jesus was sent is the same way we are sent.

So how was Jesus sent?

- Into broken systems
- Into opposing environments
- Into morally complex situations

Not to blend in, but to bring:

- Truth
- Light
- Transformation

This is where the call becomes both inspiring and demanding. Jesus was not sent into ideal circumstances. He was sent into resistance, unbelief, hypocrisy, suffering, confusion, and need. Yet He remained clear, holy, compassionate, and purposeful. If His sending becomes the pattern for ours, then we can no longer define faithfulness as staying far from complexity. Faithfulness must include learning how to carry Christ within it.

"For God did not send His Son into the world to condemn the world, but that the world through Him might be saved" (John 3:17, NKJV). His sending was redemptive. Ours must reflect that same spirit, truthful, holy, and full of purpose.

The Error of Disconnection

When believers disconnect from the world:

- They reduce their effectiveness
- They limit their reach
- They silence their influence

Because you cannot fulfill a mission in a place you refuse to enter.

This is one of the quiet failures of modern faith. Many believers want impact while remaining emotionally, relationally, or spiritually unavailable to the very people they are called to reach. But a mission does not work from a distance alone. The gospel must be embodied. Truth must be carried by people who are willing to remain present.

Disconnection may feel protective, but it often weakens the witness. It may preserve comfort, but it rarely fulfills calling. The world cannot be meaningfully influenced by believers who are absent from its hardest places.

Sanctified, Not Isolated

Jesus also prays: "Sanctify them by Your truth…", John 17:17

Sanctification is not physical distance. It is internal alignment with truth.

This means:

- Your mind is shaped by truth
- Your values are rooted in truth
- Your decisions are guided by truth

So that when you are in the world, you remain anchored.

This is such an important correction. Sanctification is not mainly about relocation; it is about consecration. It is the inward work of God that makes the believer belong to Him in mind, heart, conduct, and desire. A sanctified believer does not need to panic in every difficult setting, because his center is being formed by truth rather than by the pressure around him.

The Word of God becomes more than information here. It becomes an anchoring power. It gives the believer a way to remain steady when surroundings are unstable. It teaches him how to live in the present without becoming absorbed, and how to remain clear without becoming afraid.

The Tension We Must Embrace

Let's define the tension clearly:

- Fully engaged
- Fully anchored
- Fully present
- Fully distinct
- Fully involved
- Fully uncompromised

This is not easy. But it is necessary.

This is the Christian tension many try to escape by choosing extremes. Some choose distance so they do not have to wrestle with presence. Others choose blending in so they do not have to wrestle with distinction. But Jesus calls us to something stronger than both. He calls us to live with holy tension, present enough to serve, distinct enough to witness, and rooted enough to remain faithful.

Mature faith does not run from this tension. It grows within it. Over time, the believer learns that faithfulness is not found in oversimplified categories, but in remaining surrendered to God while living in the middle of real life.

Why Many Believers Struggle Here

Because this tension requires:

- Maturity
- Clarity
- Strong identity

Without these:

- Engagement feels risky
- Withdrawal feels safer

But safety is not the goal. Faithfulness is.

That sentence deserves to settle deeply in the heart: safety is not the goal. Faithfulness is. Many decisions that appear wise on the surface are actually driven by the deeper desire to avoid discomfort, pressure, misunderstanding, or challenge. But the believer is not ultimately called to the easiest emotional path. He is called to the obedient one.

This is why spiritual formation matters so much. The stronger a believer becomes in identity, truth, and intimacy with God, the less he will need distance to feel secure. He can remain steady because his soul has learned where to stand.

You Were Built for This Environment

Let this settle in you: God did not place you in this generation by mistake. The questions you hear, the challenges you face, and the environments you navigate are all part of your assignment. You were built for this.

This is one of the most strengthening truths a believer can receive. You are not an accidental Christian living in the wrong time. You are not misplaced in history. God was not surprised by the confusion of this age, the complexity of modern life, or the environments through which you move. He formed you with purpose and placed you in this generation knowingly.

That does not mean every challenge will feel easy. It means every challenge can become meaningful. What looks like pressure may actually be the setting where your witness becomes most necessary.

From Survival to Mission

Many believers approach life as survival, asking:

- "How do I protect myself?"
- "How do I avoid being influenced?"

But Jesus calls us to mission:

- "How do I represent Him here?"
- "How do I bring light into this space?"

This shift is critical.

Survival-centered faith always reads the environment through fear. Mission-centered faith reads the environment through purpose. One is constantly retreating inward. The other remains watchful for opportunity. This does not make the believer careless; it makes him available.

The change begins in the mind. When a believer stops seeing every challenge as a threat and starts seeing it as a place of possible representation, his whole posture shifts. He becomes more prayerful, more aware, more intentional, and more present.

The World Needs Representation, Not Retreat

The world is not lacking:

- Opinions
- Ideas
- Voices

It is lacking:

- Clear representation of truth

And that is your role.

The world has no shortage of noise. What it lacks is a clear, peaceful, grounded witness that reflects Christ honestly. That is why believers must not disappear. We are not called to add more confusion, nor merely to compete with louder voices. We are called to represent truth in a way that is stable, discerning, and deeply human.

Representation matters because many people will meet Christ through the life of a believer long before they understand Him through doctrine alone. Our presence, posture, words, patience, and conviction all become part of that witness.

A Reframing of Reality

You are not surrounded by darkness. You are positioned within opportunity.

You are not outnumbered. You are strategically placed.

You are not at risk. You are on assignment.

This reframing is powerful because it moves the believer out of fear-based imagination and into Kingdom perspective. Darkness may still be real, but it is no longer the controlling reality. Assignment becomes a stronger reality. Opposition may still exist, but purpose now speaks louder than intimidation.

When you know you are strategically placed, you stop despising where you are. You begin to ask what heaven sees there. You begin to understand that God may have positioned you in ways you have not fully appreciated yet.

The Responsibility of Being Sent

If you are sent:

- You must be prepared
- You must be intentional
- You must be aware

Because every environment becomes:

- A place of representation
- A place of influence
- A place of potential transformation

This is where calling becomes responsibility. To be sent is a privilege, but it is also a summons to maturity. The believer cannot afford to move through life half-awake, spiritually passive, or casually disconnected from his assignment. People must learn to live with prayerful awareness.

Preparation matters because opportunities often come quietly. A conversation, a question, a moment of pain in someone else, an open door in an unexpected setting, these moments can easily be missed by believers who are present physically but not present spiritually.

A Final Clarity

Let this be clear once and for all: God did not call you out of the world to remove you. He called you out to redefine you, so He could send you back.

This is one of the great movements of grace. God brings us out so He can make us new, establish our identity, cleanse our hearts, and anchor us in truth. But he does not stop there. He then sends us back into the very world we once moved through without clarity, so that now we can move through it as witnesses of another Kingdom.

That is the deeper meaning of Christian transformation. We are not only rescued from darkness. We are re-formed for mission.

Points to Ponder

1. Do I see my environment as a threat or an assignment?
2. Am I trying to escape what God has called me to engage?
3. Do I live with a sense of mission in my daily life?
4. Am I anchored enough in truth to remain steady in any environment?
5. Do I spend more energy protecting myself from the world than preparing myself to represent Christ within it?
6. Where has God already placed me that I may have been viewing with frustration instead of spiritual purpose?

7. What would change in my daily life if I truly believed I was sent and not stranded?

Call to Action

This week, shift your perspective. Wherever you go, work, conversations, environments, remind yourself: "I am sent here." Then act accordingly:

- Be intentional
- Be aware
- Be ready to represent

Before entering each setting, even briefly, pause and pray. Ask the Lord to help you see that place through the eyes of assignment. Pay attention to one conversation, one person, or one moment you might normally overlook. Let your awareness deepen. Let your posture change. Let your presence become more purposeful, more prayerful, and more responsive to God.

Declaration

I am in the world, but not of it. I am sent, not stranded. My life carries purpose in every environment. I am anchored in truth and guided by God. I do not retreat. I represent. Through me, God's presence will be revealed.

I refuse to treat my daily life as accidental, because the hand of God has placed me with purpose. I will remain present without compromise, steady without fear, and available for every assignment God places before me. The truth of God anchors me, the

Spirit of God leads me, and the mission of God gives meaning to where I stand.

Prayer

Father,

Thank you for sending me into this world with purpose. Help me to stop seeing my environment as a threat and start seeing it as an assignment. Anchor me deeply in Your truth. Protect me as I engage, and strengthen me to stand firm. Give me awareness, wisdom, and boldness. Let my life reflect Jesus in every place I go. From this day forward, I will live as one who is sent.

Lord, remove every mindset in me that keeps looking for escape when You are calling me into faithful presence. Teach me to trust Your protection, to rest in my identity, and to walk through this world with spiritual clarity. Where I have felt stranded, remind me that I am sent. Where I have felt intimidated, remind me that I am anchored in Your truth. Where I have been passive, awaken me to purpose. Let my daily life become a place where Your light, Your peace, and Your truth are carried faithfully into every environment You have entrusted to me.

In Jesus' name, Amen.

Chapter 9: Holiness Without Irrelevance

How to Remain Pure Without Becoming Powerless

This chapter addresses a tension many sincere believers quietly feel but do not always know how to explain. They want to remain holy before God, yet they also know they were not called to become invisible. Somewhere between conviction and engagement, many begin to fear that one must be sacrificed for the other.

But the life of Jesus shows us something far better. Holiness and meaningful presence do not have to compete. In Christ, they strengthen one another.

There is a quiet tension many believers live with: *If I stay holy, will I become irrelevant? If I stay relevant, will I compromise my holiness?* So they choose one side.

Some withdraw to protect purity. Others adjust to maintain a connection. But both miss the model of Jesus. Because Jesus was:

- Fully holy
- Fully relevant
- At the same time

That is what makes His life so compelling. He did not carry a holiness that pushed people away in coldness, nor a nearness that emptied truth of its substance. He moved through real human environments with a purity that never weakened and a presence that never became useless. This is the tension the believer must learn to carry with maturity.

The Two Dangerous Extremes

Let's name them clearly.

1. Holiness without Influence

This group:

- Avoids engagement
- Stays within Christian circles
- Minimizes exposure to the world

They preserve purity, but lose influence.

They are:

- Spiritually safe
- Socially absent

This kind of life may feel disciplined on the surface, yet it slowly becomes disconnected from assignment. It remains protected, but not always fruitful. It values distance more than witness, and over time, it can begin to mistake absence for faithfulness. But if no one is being touched, helped, challenged, or drawn toward truth through our lives, then something essential has been lost.

2. Relevance without Conviction

This group:

- Blends into culture
- Softens truth
- Avoids difficult topics

They maintain a connection, but lose clarity.

They are:

- Socially accepted
- Spiritually diluted

This opposite extreme is just as dangerous. It preserves access but weakens substance. It keeps the door open socially, yet often leaves little that is distinctively Christian within the room. In trying so hard not to offend, the believer may gradually stop saying anything that carries the weight of truth. Connection remains, but transforming power begins to fade.

Jesus Chose Neither Extreme

Jesus did not:

- Withdraw to remain holy
- Compromise to remain accepted

He embodied both:

- Purity without distance
- Connection without compromise

That is the standard.

This is not merely an inspiring idea. It is the pattern given to us by the Son of God. He shows us that it is possible to remain spiritually clean while being relationally present, to remain truthful while still being approachable, and to remain distinct without becoming detached. The believer is not called to choose between holiness and usefulness. In Christ, both are meant to live together.

"And the Word became flesh and dwelt among us" (John 1:14, NKJV). Even that verse carries the beauty of nearness. Holiness did not remain far away. It came near enough to be seen, heard, and encountered.

Holiness Is Not Fragile

Many believers treat holiness as if it were fragile, as if:

- One conversation
- One environment
- One interaction

will cause them to lose it.

But true holiness is not fragile. It is rooted. It comes from:

- Identity
- Conviction
- Alignment with God

Not from controlled environments.

This is an important correction. If holiness depends entirely on carefully managed surroundings, then it has not yet become strong within the soul. Biblical holiness is not a nervous state maintained only by distance. It is an inward condition shaped by God, anchored in truth, and guarded by surrender. It can remain intact even in difficult settings because its source is deeper than the environment.

Of course, wisdom still matters. Some environments require caution, and some seasons require stronger boundaries. But wisdom is different from fear. Fear says holiness cannot survive contact. Scripture shows that holiness, when deeply rooted in God, can stand where confusion exists without becoming confusion itself.

Relevance Is Not the Goal, Impact Is

Let's correct another idea. We are not called to be relevant. We are called to be effective.

Relevance seeks acceptance. Impact produces transformation.

Jesus was not always:

- Liked
- Celebrated
- Approved

But he was always:

- Clear
- Present
- Transformative

This distinction saves the believer from unnecessary pressure. We do not need to chase approval in order to matter. We do not need to appear fashionable in order to be fruitful. The goal is not to mirror the culture so perfectly that no one notices the difference. The goal is to carry something into that culture that it cannot produce on its own: truth, light, grace, and the presence of God.

Effectiveness often looks quieter than relevance. It may not draw applause, but it leaves a mark. It changes conversations, stirs conscience, opens hearts, and shifts environments over time. That is the kind of impact believers should desire.

The Power of Distinction

What makes light effective is not that it blends in. It is what stands out. If there is no difference between the believer and the environment, then there is no influence because influence requires distinction.

This is one of the simplest truths in the Christian life. A witness that looks exactly like everything around it cannot reveal anything new. Distinction is not arrogance. It is visibility. It is the quiet evidence that another Kingdom is shaping the life of the believer. Without that difference, there may be presence, but there will be little power.

Jesus said, *"Let your light so shine before men, that they may see your good works and glorify your Father in heaven"* (Matthew 5:16, NKJV). Light shines because it is not the same as the darkness around it. Its difference is part of its usefulness.

Why Some Believers Lose Their Voice

When believers try too hard to:

- Fit in
- Avoid tension
- Maintain acceptance

they begin to:

- Silence truth
- Avoid clarity
- Dilute conviction

And eventually, they lose their voice.

This loss does not usually happen all at once. It happens gradually. A believer leaves one truth unspoken, then another. One conviction becomes softened, then another becomes hidden. At first, it seems harmless, almost wise. But over time, the voice that once carried witness becomes uncertain, hesitant, and thin. The issue is not only what has been said less. It is what has slowly stopped being carried within with strength.

A believer's voice remains strong not because it is loud, but because it remains connected to conviction. Once conviction is repeatedly sacrificed for comfort, the voice begins to weaken from the inside.

Truth Must Be Clear, Not Harsh

Balance is key. We are not called to be:

- Aggressive
- Condemning
- Harsh

But neither are we called to be:

- Vague
- Silent
- Indifferent

Jesus spoke:

- Truth clearly
- With authority
- With grace

That is the model.

This balance is where many believers need maturity. Some think boldness means sharpness. Others think kindness means silence. But Jesus carried a better way. He was strong without cruelty, honest without hostility, and clear without becoming needlessly severe. The believer who follows Him must learn that truth is not weakened by gentleness, and grace is not strengthened by vagueness.

"Let your speech always be with grace, seasoned with salt" (Colossians 4:6, NKJV). That kind of speech is not soft in conviction, but it is careful in spirit. It carries both weight and warmth.

Grace and Truth Together

John 1:14 says Jesus came full of grace and truth. Not:

- Grace without truth
- Truth without grace

But both.

Truth gives clarity. Grace gives approachability. Truth tells us what is real. Grace creates room for that truth to be received without unnecessary hardness. Together, they form one of the most beautiful balances in the life of Christ. When believers carry only one without the other, representation becomes distorted.

Grace without truth may comfort people without helping them change. Truth without grace may confront people without helping them stay open. But when both are present, something powerful happens: the heart is invited, and the conscience is awakened at the same time.

This is why the believer must not only ask, *"Am I saying something true?"* but also, *"Am I carrying it in the spirit of Christ?"* Both matter.

When Purity Becomes Passivity

Some believers are so focused on avoiding compromise that they never learn how to influence. They become:

- Careful
- Reserved
- Distant

But not necessarily fruitful.

This is a sobering reality. A person can spend so much energy protecting against wrong that he forgets to practice what is right in public life. He may avoid contamination, yet never become constructive. He may remain morally cautious, yet relationally absent. At that point, holiness has not become false, but it has become incomplete in expression.

Biblical holiness is not merely defensive. It is also purposeful. It is meant to create lives strong enough to be present where light is needed.

When Relevance Becomes Conformity

Others are so focused on maintaining connection that they become difficult to distinguish. They know how to:

- Adapt
- Relate
- Blend into conversations

But over time, they become:

- Unclear
- Unconvincing
- Spiritually muted

This too must be faced honestly. The desire to connect is not wrong. In fact, it can reflect genuine compassion. But when connection becomes the highest goal, conviction often becomes negotiable. The believer begins to fear that clear truth will cost relational access, so clarity is quietly reduced. In trying to stay close to people, he may stop bringing them anything that can truly transform them.

Conformity always asks the believer to pay with something precious. Most often, it asks for the edge of conviction, the courage of clarity, and the beauty of distinction.

The Inner Strength Required

To live this balance well, a believer must be:

- Rooted in identity
- Grounded in truth
- Led by the Spirit

Without these, the pressure of the environment becomes too strong.

This is why this chapter cannot be lived by personality alone. It requires formation. It requires a secret life with God strong enough to hold the public life steady. It requires Scripture deep enough in the heart to keep the mind clear. It requires prayer deep enough to keep the soul calm. And it requires the Holy Spirit, who gives discernment for when to speak, how to stand, and how to remain pure without retreating.

"Now the Lord is the Spirit; and where the Spirit of the Lord is, there is liberty" (2 Corinthians 3:17, NKJV). That liberty includes freedom from the fear that we must either hide to remain holy or compromise to remain useful.

The Goal Is Faithful Presence

The answer is not:

- Withdrawal
- Compromise

The answer is faithful presence. A life that is:

- Holy enough to stay distinct
- Present enough to stay useful
- Clear enough to stay truthful
- Loving enough to stay connected

Faithful presence is one of the most needed qualities in the Church today. It does not disappear from difficult spaces, and it does not dissolve within them. It remains there as a witness, steady, human, prayerful, and clear. It knows how to stand without performing and how to care without surrendering what God has said.

This is the kind of life that slowly earns trust while still honoring truth. It may not satisfy every person, but it reflects Christ accurately.

The Witness of a Distinct Life

People may not immediately agree with your convictions. But they should be able to recognize:

- Your integrity
- Your consistency
- Your sincerity
- Your peace

These make holiness visible and credible.

A distinct life often speaks before words are ever fully heard. People notice when someone is clean in motive, stable under pressure, gentle in tone, and consistent over time. They may resist the message at first, but they often remember the life that carried it. This is why the witness of holiness must be lived, not merely claimed.

1 Peter 2:12 gives a powerful reminder: *"having your conduct honorable among the Gentiles"* (NKJV). Conduct matters because it gives the message a visible form.

A Needed Reframing

Do not ask, *"How close can I get without compromising?"* And do not ask, *"How much can I soften and still be accepted?"*

Ask instead, *"How can I represent Christ here with both purity and power?"*

That question changes the whole direction of the heart. It moves us away from the anxious calculations of self-protection and social approval. It brings us back to the mission. The issue is no longer merely what to avoid or how to be liked. The issue becomes how to reveal Christ faithfully in the place where we stand.

A Call to Maturity

The mature believer learns:

- How to stay clean in a messy world
- How to stay clear in a confused world
- How to stay kind without becoming weak
- How to stay firm without becoming harsh

This is maturity.

And maturity is beautiful because it makes the believer useful. It does not merely preserve his private life; it strengthens his public witness. It gives him the ability to move through real spaces with a heart that is guarded by God and a life that remains available to God.

Points to Ponder

1. Am I leaning more toward withdrawal or compromise?
2. Have I mistaken holiness for distance?
3. Have I mistaken relevance for acceptance?
4. Does my life carry both truth and grace?
5. In what situations do I feel the strongest pressure either to hide my convictions or to soften them?
6. Is my present way of living making Christ more visible, or less visible, to the people around me?
7. What area of my life needs deeper spiritual rooting so I can remain both pure and useful?

Call to Action

This week, examine one environment where you tend to struggle:

- A workplace
- A friendship
- A conversation space

Ask yourself, *"How can I remain fully Christlike here, without withdrawing, and without blending in?"* Then practice one intentional response.

Let that response be simple and sincere. It may be a clear word, a firm boundary, a gracious answer, a quiet refusal to compromise, or a more intentional presence than usual. Do not aim to impress. Aim to represent Christ well. Let one real act of faithful presence become the beginning of stronger maturity.

Declaration

I walk in holiness without becoming irrelevant. I remain pure without withdrawing. I remain present without compromising. I carry both grace and truth. My life is distinct, useful, and effective. Through me, Christ will be seen clearly.

I do not need to choose between purity and impact, because in Christ I am called to live with both.

My convictions remain firm, my spirit remains tender, and my witness remains visible. The life of God in me will not fade in the presence of pressure; it will shine with greater clarity.

Prayer

Father,

Thank you for calling me to live a life that is both holy and useful. Keep me from the extremes of withdrawal and compromise. Strengthen my identity so that I do not fear difficult environments. Anchor me in truth so that I do not lose clarity. Fill me with grace so that I reflect Christ well.

Teach me how to remain pure without becoming distant, and how to remain present without becoming diluted. Let my life carry both conviction and compassion. Let my witness remain clear, credible, and full of light.

Lord, make my holiness deep, steady, and alive. Do not let it become a fearful distance from people, and do not let my desire to connect with people weaken what You have formed in me. Teach me how to walk through this world with a clean heart, a clear mind, and a spirit that remains full of both truth and grace. Where I have hidden to protect myself, strengthen me. Where I have softened truth to preserve acceptance, correct me. Let my life reflect the beauty of

Christ so faithfully that others can see both purity and love living together in me.

In Jesus' name,

Amen.

Chapter 10: Why Do You Believe?

Moving from Assumed Faith to Articulated Conviction

There comes a moment in the life of nearly every believer when faith is no longer carried only in worship, prayer, or private devotion. It is brought into conversation. It is examined by a question. It is pulled into the open by someone who genuinely wants to know, or by someone who quietly doubts that there is anything solid beneath what we say we believe.

This chapter speaks to that moment. It is not meant to pressure the believer into performance, but to awaken a needed maturity. Faith should live in the heart, yes, but it should also be able to find honest, thoughtful, human words.

At some point, every believer will face a moment like this:

- A friend asks
- A colleague challenges
- A skeptic questions: *"Why do you believe in Jesus?"*

And at that moment, everything is revealed.

Not your passion. Not your church attendance. Not your spiritual activity. But your clarity.

That is why this question matters so deeply. It reaches beyond emotion and touches formation. A person may be sincere, devoted, and spiritually active, yet still feel strangely unsteady when asked to explain what they believe. In that moment, faith is not being measured by volume, but by understanding, not by how moved we feel, but by whether conviction has become clear enough to be expressed.

The Silence That Should Not Exist

Many believers freeze in that moment. Not because they do not believe, but because they have never learned to express what they believe.

So they respond with:

- "I just have faith…"
- "It's personal…"
- "That's what I grew up with…"

And while these answers may be honest, they are not sufficient. Because they do not:

- Explain
- Clarify
- Invite understanding

These kinds of responses often come from real sincerity, but they leave too much unspoken. They may protect a believer from immediate discomfort, yet they do not help the listener understand the reason for our hope. A quiet answer may feel safer in the moment, but over time, it can reinforce the idea that Christian faith is vague, inherited, or emotionally driven without substance. This is one reason the Church must help believers move beyond instinctive language into thoughtful expression.

Faith Must Be Personal, But Not Private

Faith is personal. But it was never meant to be private.

"Always be prepared to give an answer…", 1 Peter 3:15

This is not a suggestion. It is a responsibility.

God expects believers to be:

- Ready
- Clear
- Able to respond

This verse gives dignity to preparation. God does not ask His people to speak from panic, confusion, or borrowed phrases alone. He calls us to readiness. That means our faith should be loved deeply enough to be studied, understood, and explained. Personal faith is precious, but private faith alone is incomplete when Christ has called us to represent Him openly in the world.

"But sanctify the Lord God in your hearts, and always be ready to give a defense to everyone who asks you a reason for the hope that is in you" (1 Peter 3:15, NKJV)

Notice that readiness begins in the heart, but it does not stay there. What is sanctified inwardly must eventually become expressible outwardly.

Why This Question Matters

"Why do you believe?" is not just a question. It is an invitation, an opportunity to:

- Reveal truth
- Clarify misconceptions
- Open a door

But if you are unprepared, the opportunity is lost.

Sometimes that question comes from skepticism. Sometimes it comes from pain. Sometimes it comes from quiet hunger. Sometimes it comes from a person who has seen enough inconsistency in religion that he now wonders whether there is anything real left to trust. In every case, the question creates an opening. The believer does not need to fear that opening. He needs to be formed enough to step into it with peace.

The Difference Between Knowing and Explaining

You may know something internally, yet struggle to explain it externally. That gap must be closed.

Because if you cannot explain your faith, you cannot share it effectively.

Many believers truly do know Christ, love Christ, and trust Christ. The issue is not always the absence of faith. The issue is often the absence of articulation. They have inward assurance, but not yet outward clarity. This does not make their faith false, but it does make their witness weaker than it should be. God desires that what is real within us become understandable through us.

A Simple, Clear Foundation

Every believer should be able to answer three core questions:

1. Why Do You Believe in God?

Not only emotionally, but rationally and personally.

- The existence of order, design, and purpose
- The reality of moral law
- Personal encounter and conviction

These points matter because faith in God is not an irrational surrender to emptiness. The believer can point to the meaningful order of creation, the moral awareness written deeply into human life, and the inward conviction that grows through encounter with

God. Not every answer has to sound academic. It does, however, need to sound thoughtful, honest, and grounded.

2. Why Jesus?

This is the central question.

- His life, teachings, and impact
- His death and resurrection
- The uniqueness of His claims

Jesus is not just:

- A teacher
- A prophet
- A moral example

He is:

- The Son of God
- The only way to reconciliation

This is where Christian faith becomes unmistakably centered. We do not merely admire Jesus. We trust Him as Lord. We do not simply borrow His ethics. We believe His person, His cross, His resurrection, and His claims change everything. This is why the believer must become increasingly clear here. If Jesus is reduced to inspiration alone, the gospel loses its center.

Jesus said, *"I am the way, the truth, and the life. No one comes to the Father except through Me"* (John 14:6, NKJV). That statement does not leave room for a vague Christ. It calls for a clear one.

3. Why the Bible?

- Its consistency across time
- Its prophetic accuracy
- Its transformative power

You do not need to be a scholar. But you must have clarity.

The believer does not need to answer every question about Scripture at once, but he should know why he trusts it. The Bible is not merely an ancient religious text preserved by habit. It is the living Word through which God reveals truth, exposes the heart, and transforms lives. Many believers have experienced its power personally, but they must also learn how to speak about that trust with steadiness and simplicity.

"For the word of God is living and powerful, and sharper than any two-edged sword" (Hebrews 4:12, NKJV). Scripture is not powerful only when preached from a pulpit. It remains powerful when trusted, understood, and explained through the life of a believer.

Clarity Over Complexity

You do not need:

- Big words
- Complex arguments
- Philosophical depth

You need:

- Clear thinking
- Simple explanation
- Honest conviction

Why? Because clarity connects.

This frees many believers immediately. God is not asking everyone to become a public apologist or academic thinker in form. He is asking for understandable faith. The most powerful answers are often not the most complicated. They are the most sincere, the most coherent, and the most grounded in truth. People often hear simple clarity more deeply than impressive language.

Jesus' Way of Explaining Truth

Jesus did not overwhelm people. He:

- Used stories
- Asked questions
- Gave clear illustrations

He made truth:

- Understandable
- Accessible
- Relatable

You must do the same.

There is wisdom in the way Jesus spoke. He did not use complexity to create distance. He spoke in a way that reached hearts and minds together. He drew from life, from fields, seeds, lamps, bread, sheep, fathers, and sons. He made truth feel near enough to be grasped. This should challenge believers who think clarity is too simple to be powerful. In Christ, simplicity often became the doorway into deep revelation.

Answering Without Arguing

This is critical. Your goal is not to:

- Win arguments
- Prove superiority
- Silence others

Your goal is to:

- Present truth clearly
- Invite reflection
- Create space for thought

This protects the believer from a common mistake. Once someone begins to grow in understanding, there can be a temptation to use truth like a weapon of control rather than a means of witness. But Christ did not call us to dominate conversations. He called us to represent Him faithfully. The goal is not to leave the other person humiliated. The goal is to leave truth present in the room in a way that can still work on the heart after the conversation ends.

Confidence Without Arrogance

When you know why you believe:

- You are not defensive
- You are not aggressive
- You are not intimidated

You are:

- Calm
- Clear
- Grounded

Because truth does not need aggression, it needs clarity.

There is a holy steadiness that grows in the believer when understanding deepens. He no longer needs to panic when questioned. He no longer needs to force his voice to sound stronger than his soul feels. He becomes calmer because he is more rooted. This kind of confidence is beautiful because it does not come from pride. It comes from settled conviction.

"The servant of the Lord must not quarrel but be gentle to all, able to teach, patient" (2 Timothy 2:24, NKJV). That is not weak faith. It is mature faith.

What If You Don't Know?

Let's be practical. You will not always have every answer. And that is okay.

But instead of:

- Avoiding
- Deflecting

You can say: *"That's a great question. Let me look into that."* And then follow up.

Growth happens when:

- You acknowledge gaps
- You pursue understanding

This is an important kind of honesty. The believer does not have to pretend to know what he has not yet learned. Pretending may protect pride for a moment, but humility builds a stronger witness over time. There is strength in saying, with sincerity, that you are still learning. What matters is whether you remain teachable, hungry, and willing to return with greater clarity.

The Danger of Unexamined Faith

If you never ask yourself, *"Why do I believe?"* then your faith remains:

- Inherited
- Unexamined
- Vulnerable

But when you examine it, it becomes:

- Personal
- Grounded
- Unshakable

This is where many believers need to slow down and become honest. It is possible to grow up around Christian language without ever deeply wrestling with Christian conviction. It is possible to inherit a faith environment without yet owning the faith itself, with understanding. But once a believer begins to examine what he believes before God, not with rebellion, but with sincerity, faith often becomes stronger, deeper, and more durable.

From Passive Believer to Active Witness

When clarity is developed:

- Conversations become opportunities
- Questions become openings
- Engagement becomes natural

You move from:

- Avoiding discussions

to:

- Entering them with purpose

That is a beautiful shift. The believer stops seeing every question as a threat and starts recognizing it as a moment of possible ministry. What once produced hesitation now begins to awaken readiness. Not because all nervousness disappears, but because conviction has grown sturdy enough to stand.

Your Story Still Matters

While explanation is important, never forget that your personal testimony is powerful. Not as a replacement for truth, but as a confirmation of it.

People may debate ideas, but they cannot deny transformation.

A testimony becomes especially powerful when it is joined to clarity. It shows that the truth being spoken is not merely a theory carried in the mind, but a reality that has touched a life. The believer should never treat his story as the whole argument, but neither should he underestimate it. A changed life gives human weight to the message it proclaims.

"And they overcame him by the blood of the Lamb and by the word of their testimony" (Revelation 12:11, NKJV). Testimony does not replace truth. It bears witness to what truth has done.

A Prepared Believer Is a Confident Believer

Preparation removes fear. When you know:

- What you believe
- Why do you believe
- How to explain it

You no longer:

- Avoid conversations
- Fear questions
- Withdraw from engagement

You step in.

Preparation does not make a believer perfect, but it does make him more available. He can listen better, answer more wisely, and remain calmer under pressure. The soul becomes less fragile when the foundation becomes more understood. This is one reason preparation is not optional maturity. It is part of being ready for the world Christ has sent us into.

A Necessary Shift

The Church must move from *"Just believe"* to *"Understand and be ready to explain."*

This shift is not a move away from faith. It is a move toward stronger faith. It is the difference between carrying Christian language and carrying Christian conviction. A believer should not only know that Jesus matters. He should increasingly know how to say why He matters.

The Responsibility of Representation

You represent Christ, and representation requires:

- Clarity
- Understanding
- Readiness

Because people will not read the Bible first. They will read:

- Your words
- Your explanations
- Your responses

This is one of the sobering realities of witness. For many people, the first interpretation of Christianity they meet is not a sermon, but a believer. Not a commentary, but a conversation. Not a theological text, but an answer. That means the way we explain our faith matters deeply. Our words do not save anyone, but they can either illuminate truth or make it seem farther away than it really is.

A Final Challenge

If someone asked you today, *"Why do you believe in Jesus?"* could you answer:

- Clearly?
- Simply?
- Confidently?

If not, this is where your growth begins.

And that growth does not begin in shame. It begins in honesty. The Lord is not condemning the believer who has not yet learned how to answer well. He is inviting that believer into deeper strength. This chapter is not a verdict against weakness. It is a call toward maturity.

Points to Ponder

1. Can I clearly explain why I believe in Jesus?
2. What parts of my faith do I struggle to explain?
3. Do I avoid questions, or embrace them?
4. Am I actively growing in understanding?
5. Have I confused sincere belief with prepared belief?

6. What would I say today if someone asked me why Jesus is the center of my life?
7. Where do I need to grow so my faith can be expressed with greater peace, clarity, and conviction?

Call to Action

Write your answer to this question: *"Why do I believe in Jesus?"* Keep it:

* Clear
* Simple
* Honest

Practice saying it out loud. Refine it until it flows naturally.

Then take one step further. Write down three short answers as well: why you believe in God, why you trust Jesus, and why you believe the Bible is true. Do not aim for polished language first. Aim for truthful language. Read it aloud. Pray over it. Keep working until your answer sounds like you, clear, grounded, and real.

Declaration

I know what I believe and why I believe it. I am not intimidated by questions. I speak truth with clarity and confidence. I represent Christ with wisdom and grace. My words carry truth that brings light to others. Through me, people will encounter understanding.

I will not hide behind vague language when God is calling me into clearer conviction. My faith is becoming stronger, deeper, and more articulate. The truth of Christ in me will be expressed with humility, peace, and courage.

Prayer

Father,

Thank You for the gift of faith. Now give me understanding to support it. Teach me how to explain what I believe clearly. Remove every fear of questions and challenges. Give me wisdom, clarity, and confidence. Let my words reflect truth and draw others to You. From this day forward, I will be ready.

Lord, deepen what is true in me until it becomes steady in my speech. Where I have believed sincerely but spoken uncertainly, strengthen me. Where I have hidden behind silence because I did not know what to say, teach me patiently. Give me a love for truth that is humble, thoughtful, and alive. Help me not merely to repeat what I have heard, but to understand what I believe and why it matters. Let my testimony be honest, my mind be formed by Your Word, and my answers be marked by grace. When questions come, let fear not govern me. Let Christ be clearly seen in both my conviction and my tone.

In Jesus' name,

Amen.

Chapter 11: Engaging Opposing Worldviews

How to Stand Firm Without Becoming Defensive or Silent

This chapter enters one of the most practical realities of Christian witness. It is one thing to believe sincerely in private, and another thing to remain clear when your beliefs are questioned in real time. Many believers do not fail in these moments because they do not love God. They struggle because pressure exposes what has not yet been deeply formed. But opposing worldviews do not have to become moments of panic. In Christ, they can become moments of wise, calm, Spirit-led engagement.

At some point, every believer will encounter it: a conversation that challenges everything they believe. Not in church. Not in a safe environment. But in real life:

• At work.
• In school.
• In friendships.
• In public conversations.

And in those moments, many believers do one of three things:

1.   They avoid.
2.   They become defensive.
3.   Or they remain silent.

None of these lead to influence.

These reactions are understandable, but they are not the goal of maturity. Avoidance protects comfort. Defensiveness protects ego.

Silence protects us from exposure. Yet none of them truly serve the person in front of us, and none of them fully represent Christ. The Lord calls us into something deeper than self-protection. He calls us into faithful presence.

Opposition Is Not the Enemy

Let's start here. Opposing views are not a problem. They are an opportunity. Because:

• Questions reveal curiosity.
• Disagreement reveals engagement.
• Resistance often hides deeper searching.

If there were no opposing views…there would be no need for light.

This shift in perspective matters deeply. The believer who sees opposition only as a threat will approach every difficult conversation with tension before it even begins. But the believer who sees opposition as an opening will begin to listen more carefully and respond more wisely. Not every challenging voice is hostile at its core. Sometimes disagreement is simply the doorway through which a deeper hunger begins to speak.

Scripture reminds us, "And a servant of the Lord must not quarrel but be gentle to all, able to teach, patient" (2 Timothy 2:24, NKJV). That verse assumes that believers will face resistance. But it also shows us the spirit with which resistance should be met.

Why Many Believers Struggle in These Moments

Because they are:

• Emotionally unprepared.
• Intellectually untrained.
• Spiritually uncertain.

So when pressure comes, they feel:

• Cornered.
• Overwhelmed.
• Insecure.

And instead of engaging…they retreat.

This is why preparation matters so much. Pressure does not usually create weakness; it reveals it. A believer who has not learned how to think clearly, remain emotionally steady, and rest in identity will often feel exposed the moment opposition appears. Yet this chapter is not meant to shame that weakness. It is meant to expose it gently so it can be strengthened.

The Goal of Engagement

Let's clarify something important. The goal is not:

• To win debates.
• To dominate conversations.
• To prove others wrong.

The goal is: to represent truth clearly, confidently, and respectfully.

That distinction protects the believer from two common traps: pride and fear. Pride wants to conquer the other person. Fear wants to escape the moment. But love seeks something better. Love wants truth to be heard, dignity to be preserved, and the person before us to remain reachable. Christian engagement is not verbal combat. It is faithful representation.

Start With Listening, Not Speaking

Most believers make this mistake: they respond before they understand. But effective engagement begins with listening. So…

• What is the person actually saying?
• What do they really believe?
• What is driving their perspective?

When you listen:

• You gain clarity.
• You build trust.
• You avoid unnecessary conflict.

Listening is not weakness. It is one of the most intelligent forms of strength in conversation. It slows down reaction, uncovers motives, and often reveals that the person's real issue is deeper than the first statement they made. Sometimes a person sounds argumentative, but beneath that argument there may be disappointment, confusion, pain, or a distorted picture of God. Listening helps us respond to the real issue, not just the loudest sentence.

James 1:19 offers simple wisdom that remains powerful: "Let every man be swift to hear, slow to speak, slow to wrath" (NKJV). In difficult conversations, that order matters.

Ask Questions Before Giving Answers

Jesus often responded with questions. Why? Because questions:

• Reveal deeper thinking.
• Expose assumptions.
• Invite reflection.

Instead of rushing to answer, ask:

• "What do you mean by that?"
• "Why do you see it that way?"
• "What led you to that conclusion?"

This shifts the conversation from:

• Confrontation.

to

• Exploration.

Questions create space. They slow the emotional pace of the conversation and help both people move beneath surface reactions. They also keep the believer from answering a simplified version of what the other person is actually wrestling with. Wise questions do not weaken truth. They often make truth easier to receive because they invite the other person to examine what they are saying instead of merely defending it.

Stay Calm Under Pressure

When conversations become tense:

• Do not react emotionally.
• Do not raise your tone.
• Do not become defensive.

Because the moment you lose composure…you lose influence.

Calmness communicates confidence.

Calmness is one of the clearest signs that identity is doing its work. When a believer is deeply rooted in Christ, he does not need to panic because someone disagrees. He can remain steady without becoming cold, and clear without becoming sharp. Emotional control does not mean the conversation means nothing. It means the conversation will not be ruled by the flesh.

"A soft answer turns away wrath, but a harsh word stirs up anger" (Proverbs 15:1, NKJV). That is not merely poetic wisdom. It is practical guidance for real conversations.

You Don't Need to Win Every Point

Let this free you. You are not responsible for:

• Convincing everyone.
• Answering everything perfectly.

Your responsibility is:

• To be faithful.
• To be clear.
• To represent truth well.

God handles the rest.

This brings a holy relief to the believer. You do not have to carry the burden of changing hearts by force. That work belongs to God. Your role is to remain available, truthful, prayerful, and sincere. Sometimes a conversation will not end with agreement, but that does not mean it was fruitless. A seed may have been planted. A false assumption may have been unsettled. A door may have remained open because you stayed gracious.

Common Conversations You Will Face

Let's be practical.

1. "All religions are the same."

Response:

• Acknowledge the desire for unity.
• Clarify that beliefs make different truth claims.
• Gently show why Jesus is unique.

This is an important place for gentleness and clarity. Many who say this are not always making a careful theological statement. Sometimes they are expressing a desire for peace or fairness. That is why the believer should respond with patience. Yet peace cannot be built on pretending all truth claims say the same thing when they clearly do not. The uniqueness of Jesus must be spoken with both humility and confidence.

Jesus said, "I am the way, the truth, and the life. No one comes to the Father except through Me" (John 14:6, NKJV). His claim is not one option among many. It is a defining claim.

2. "There is no absolute truth."

Response:

• Ask: "Is that statement absolutely true?"
• Help them see the contradiction.

This kind of response is helpful because it does not mock the person. It simply exposes the instability of the statement itself. Sometimes people need to hear their own assumption more clearly before they can recognize where it breaks down.

3. "Why does God allow suffering?"

Response:

• Acknowledge the reality of pain.
• Avoid shallow answers.
• Show that Christianity does not ignore suffering—it addresses it through redemption.

This question should never be answered carelessly. It often comes from wounds, loss, disappointment, or grief, not mere philosophy. The believer must slow down here and respond with tenderness. Christianity does not deny the ache of suffering. It speaks into it with the reality of a God who enters human pain, bears the cross, and promises final restoration.

"The Lord is near to those who have a broken heart" (Psalms 34:18, NKJV). That truth matters when abstract questions are carrying personal tears underneath them.

4. "Science has replaced God."

Response:

• Clarify that science explains processes, not ultimate purpose.
• Show that belief in God and scientific discovery are not opposites.

The believer should not sound threatened by this question. Science, rightly understood, examines aspects of creation. It does not erase the Creator. Explaining how things function is not the same as explaining why anything exists at all, why order is intelligible, or why meaning continues to press on the human soul.

Truth Must Be Delivered with Wisdom

Even correct answers can be ineffective if delivered poorly. Truth must be:

• Timely.
• Thoughtful.
• Respectful…because delivery affects reception.

This is one of the most overlooked lessons in spiritual maturity. A true statement spoken at the wrong moment, in the wrong spirit, or with unnecessary force can harden the atmosphere. Wisdom helps truth arrive in a way that can still be heard. This is not compromise. It is stewardship of influence.

Respect the Person, Challenge the Idea

Never confuse the two. People deserve respect. Ideas must be examined.

So you can:

• Honor the individual while addressing the belief.

Without:

• Attacking.
• Dismissing.
• Disrespecting.

This distinction is precious. Once a believer begins to confuse a person with the worldview they hold, conversations become harsher than they need to be. But every human being bears dignity, even when carrying ideas that are false, broken, or dangerous. We can challenge error without dishonoring the image-bearer standing before us.

Your Life Must Support Your Words

If your life:

Contradicts your message, your words lose power. But when your life:

• Reflects integrity.
• Demonstrates consistency.

Your words gain weight. A life of integrity gives visible support to verbal witness. People may question what you believe, but they are often watching how you live long before they fully process what you say. Consistency does not make you perfect. It makes your message more credible.

Jesus taught, "Let your light so shine before men, that they may see your good works and glorify your Father in heaven" (Matthew 5:16, NKJV). Light is seen not only in speech, but in conduct.

Engagement Requires Patience

Transformation rarely happens in one conversation. It is:

• A process.
• A journey.
• A series of moments.

Your role is not to:

• Finish the work.
• But to…
• Be part of the process.

This helps believers stay hopeful and humble. Not every meaningful conversation ends dramatically. Sometimes the most important thing you do is remain gracious enough that the person is willing to think again later. Patience keeps us from trying to force spiritual outcomes in one moment that God may unfold over time.

Do Not Fear Being Challenged

Being challenged does not weaken your faith. It strengthens it because it forces you to:

• Think.
• Grow.
• Refine your understanding.

Avoiding challenge leads to stagnation. Engaging leads to maturity.

This is one reason believers should stop treating challenge as an interruption to spiritual life. It can become part of spiritual development. Questions press us into deeper study. Objections expose weak spots in understanding. Opposition can reveal where conviction must become clearer and stronger.

The Role of the Holy Spirit

Never forget this: you are not alone in these conversations. The Holy Spirit:

• Guides.
• Reminds.
• Gives wisdom.

You are responsible for:

• Being prepared.

God is responsible for:

• Touching hearts.

This truth brings both comfort and sobriety. We are called to prepare, but never to depend on preparation alone. The Spirit of God can guide a word, check a tone, bring Scripture to remembrance, and give unusual discernment in a moment. Conversation is not merely intellectual activity for the believer. It is also spiritual stewardship.

Jesus said, "For the Holy Spirit will teach you in that very hour what you ought to say" (Luke 12:12, NKJV). That does not cancel preparation. It sanctifies it with dependence.

A Shift in Mindset

• Move from: "I hope this doesn't happen...."

to

• "I am ready when it does."

Because engagement is not an interruption. It is part of your assignment.

This mindset changes how daily life is approached. The believer stops seeing difficult conversations as unwelcome intrusions and starts recognizing them as part of his calling. Readiness becomes an act of obedience, not anxiety.

The Confidence of a Prepared Believer

When you are:

• Grounded in identity.
• Clear in understanding.
• Practiced in engagement.

You no longer:

• Fear conversations.
• Avoid opposing views.
• Remain silent.

You step in with:

• Calmness.
• Clarity.
• Confidence.

This kind of confidence is not loud. It is steady. It does not need to overpower a room. It simply remains present without collapsing. That is often where witness becomes strongest—when a believer's steadiness reveals that truth has become settled within him.

A Final Perspective

People are not your enemies. They are:

• Searching.
• Questioning.
• Processing.
• Even when they resist.

And your role is not to defeat them.

It is to:

• Engage them.
• Respect them.
• Point them toward truth.

This final perspective protects the heart of the believer. Once we begin seeing people as opponents to crush, our tone hardens and our witness shrinks. But when we remember that many who resist are still wrestling internally, we are more likely to carry truth in a way that leaves room for grace to work.

Points To Ponder

1. How do I typically respond when my beliefs are challenged?
2. Do I listen well—or react quickly?
3. Am I prepared to handle common objections?
4. Do I approach conversations with fear—or with purpose?
5. Do I treat difficult conversations as threats, or as moments where God may be inviting me to grow and represent Him more faithfully?

6. What part of me becomes most unstable when opposition appears—my emotions, my understanding, or my confidence?

7. How would my conversations change if I remembered more deeply that people are not my enemies?

Call To Action

This week, practice one conversation skill:

• Ask more questions.
• Listen more carefully.
• Respond more thoughtfully.
• Focus on understanding before answering.

Choose one real conversation where you normally would have rushed, reacted, or withdrawn. Enter it prayerfully. Slow your pace. Let the other person speak fully. Ask a sincere question before offering your view. Afterward, reflect honestly on what happened. Notice where you felt defensive, where grace helped you remain steady, and where you still need growth.

Declaration

I engage with wisdom and confidence. I am not intimidated by opposing views. I listen with understanding and speak with clarity. I represent truth with grace and respect. I am prepared for every conversation God brings my way. Through me, truth will be heard and considered.

I do not fear disagreement, because my identity is rooted in Christ and my mind is being formed by truth. I will not answer from panic, pride, or insecurity, but from calm conviction and love. God will use my words, my tone, and my presence to make room for truth to be heard.

Prayer

Father,

Thank You for the opportunity to represent You in conversations. Teach me how to engage with wisdom, patience, and clarity. Help me to listen well and respond with grace. Remove every fear of opposition and replace it with confidence.

Guide my words and my thoughts. Let every conversation become an opportunity for truth to be revealed.

Lord, steady me in every place where I have felt intimidated by disagreement. Heal the inward fear that has made me silent, sharp, or withdrawn. Teach me how to carry truth with the spirit of Christ—firm, gentle, clear, and unafraid. Give me discernment to know when to speak, when to ask, when to wait, and when to let a few faithful words do their work. Let my life support my message, and let my message reflect Your heart. In every difficult conversation, remind me that I am not alone. Let Your Spirit guide me so that I may speak with wisdom, listen with compassion, and leave behind something that points others toward You. In Jesus' name, Amen.

Chapter 12: Truth Without Hostility

Why Tone, Attitude, and Spirit Matter as Much as Content

There are moments when a believer can say the right thing and still leave the wrong impression. Not because the truth was false, but because the spirit behind it did not reflect Christ. This chapter addresses that hidden but very important part of Christian witness. Many believers work hard to learn what to say, yet give far less attention to how truth sounds when it leaves their mouths. But heaven cares about both. Truth must not only be accurate. It must also be carried in a way that reflects the heart of the One who is Truth Himself.

There is a mistake many believers make when defending their faith: they focus entirely on what to say, but ignore how they say it. And yet, in most conversations, tone speaks before content is even processed.

You can carry truth, but if it is delivered with:

- Harshness
- Pride
- Impatience

It will often be rejected, not because it is wrong, but because it is poorly represented.

This is one of the quiet tragedies of Christian communication. A believer may hold a sound conviction, a biblical answer, even a necessary correction, and still fail to make room for truth to be heard because the posture of the heart was wrong in the moment. People often hear attitude before they absorb content. They feel contempt before they can consider meaning. That is why the spirit of our speech cannot be treated as a minor detail. It is part of our witness.

Right Message, Wrong Spirit

It is possible to:

- Be correct
- Be biblical
- Be logically sound

…and still push people away.

Why? Because truth, when delivered with the wrong spirit, feels like:

- Attack instead of invitation
- Condemnation instead of clarity
- Superiority instead of service

And people do not just respond to your words. They respond to your spirit.

This does not mean people will always accept the truth if it is delivered well. Some will still resist. Some will still reject. But the believer must make sure that rejection, when it comes, is because of the truth itself and not because of unnecessary harshness, ego, or impatience. We must not add flesh to what God intended to carry life.

Scripture gives us a needed balance here: *"Speaking the truth in love"* (Ephesians 4:15, NKJV). Truth without love becomes difficult to receive. Love without truth becomes unwilling to help. God calls us to carry both together.

Jesus: Strong Truth, Gentle Delivery

Jesus never compromised truth. But he also never:

- Belittled people
- Spoke with arrogance
- Reacted with insecurity

He could:

- Correct firmly
- Speak directly
- Challenge deeply

Yet still:

- Draw people
- Engage hearts
- Create space for transformation

This is one of the most beautiful marks of the life of Jesus. He was never vague, yet He was never small in spirit. He could expose hypocrisy without becoming cruel. He could confront sin without losing compassion. He could speak the hard truth and still leave open a door for repentance. His words carried weight because His spirit remained pure.

Even when He spoke strongly, there was purpose in it, not irritation for its own sake. He was not trying to prove himself. He was revealing the Father. That is the model the believer must recover in a world where loudness is often mistaken for strength.

Why Hostility Appears

Let's be honest. Hostility often comes from:

- Insecurity
- Frustration
- Lack of understanding
- Feeling threatened

When a believer feels:

- Cornered
- Unprepared
- Challenged

They may respond with:

- Aggression
- Sarcasm
- Dismissiveness

Not because they are strong, but because they are uncomfortable.

This is why tone is not merely a communication issue. It is often a spiritual mirror. It reveals what is happening inside us while we speak. A sharp response may say more about our insecurity than about our conviction. A sarcastic response may reveal inward fear, bruised pride, or lack of preparation. Sometimes what sounds like boldness is simply discomfort wearing a harder face.

The Lord does not expose this to shame us, but to mature us. He wants our convictions to become strong enough that we no longer need aggression to protect them.

Calmness Is a Sign of Confidence

A confident believer:

- Does not rush
- Does not react emotionally
- Does not feel the need to dominate

They:

- Listen
- Process
- Respond with clarity

Because they know the truth does not need to be forced. It needs to be presented.

There is something deeply powerful about calm conviction. It tells the room that your faith is not built on panic. It reveals that your identity is not collapsing under disagreement. A believer who stays steady under pressure often says more through composure than another says through ten loud sentences.

"A soft answer turns away wrath, but a harsh word stirs up anger" (Proverbs 15:1, NKJV). That is not a weakness. It is spiritual wisdom. Calmness is often one of the clearest forms of strength.

Your Tone Determines Your Reach

You may be speaking the truth, but if your tone communicates:

- Judgment
- Pride
- Irritation

You will lose access to the person.

Because people close their hearts before they consider your words.

This is painful but real. A person may still remember your sentence long after the conversation ends, but what stays with them most strongly may be how you made them feel while saying it. If they feel talked down to, cornered, or treated like a problem instead of a person, their heart often shuts before truth has had room to do its deeper work.

Reach is not only about being heard. It is about remaining receivable. Tone plays a large role in that.

Grace Is Not Weakness

Some fear that being gentle means being weak. That is not true. Grace is:

- Strength under control
- Truth expressed with care
- Authority without aggression

Jesus demonstrated this perfectly.

Grace does not weaken truth. It dignifies truth. It carries truth in a form that reflects the character of Christ. Some believers speak harshly because they fear gentleness will make them sound uncertain. But heaven does not measure strength by sharpness. Strength is often seen most clearly in restraint, in self-control, in measured words, and in a spirit that remains clean under pressure.

"Let your speech always be with grace, seasoned with salt" (Colossians 4:6, NKJV). Grace-filled speech does not remove conviction. It makes conviction more useful.

Speak to Win the Person, Not the Argument

This is a major shift. If your goal is to win the argument, you may:

- Push harder
- Speak sharper
- Try to corner the other person

But if your goal is to win the person, you will:

- Stay patient
- Stay respectful
- Stay thoughtful

And that changes everything.

This is where motive matters. Why are you speaking? Why are you responding? Why are you pressing the point? If your hidden goal is to prove yourself right, pride will quietly shape your delivery. But if your goal is to represent Christ and leave room for truth to reach the heart, your tone will often become more patient, more careful, and more human.

The believer must remember that conversations are not battlefields for ego. They are opportunities for witness.

Timing Matters

Not every moment is the right moment. Sometimes:

- The person is not ready
- The environment is not appropriate
- The conversation is not open

Wisdom knows:

- When to speak
- When to pause
- When to wait

Maturity includes discernment. Not every truth must be delivered in its fullest form in every moment. Sometimes the wisest response is brief. Sometimes it is a question. Sometimes it is silence that preserves dignity and leaves the door open for another day. This is not a compromise. It is spiritual sensitivity.

Jesus Himself did not answer every person the same way. He understood timing, motive, openness, and context. The believer must learn that same wisdom.

Words Should Build, Not Break

Even when correcting, your words should:

- Clarify
- Invite
- Challenge constructively

Not:

- Humiliate
- Dismiss
- Shut down

Correction is most powerful when it still honors the humanity of the person receiving it. We are not called to crush people with truth, but to bring truth in a way that can awaken, invite, and redirect. There are times when a hard word is necessary, but even then, it should not be driven by cruelty.

2 Timothy 2:25 speaks of *"correcting those who are in opposition"* (NKJV), but it places that correction in humility. That means even our strongest moments should still reflect the spirit of Christ.

Emotional Control Is Spiritual Maturity

If your emotions:

- Rise quickly
- Take over easily
- Control your response

Then your effectiveness will be limited.

Maturity looks like:

- Staying steady
- Staying composed
- Staying focused

Even under pressure.

This is an area where many sincere believers still need growth. Passion is not the same as maturity. Strong feelings do not automatically produce a strong witness. In fact, when emotions take over too easily, they often blur discernment and weaken clarity. The believer must learn how to feel deeply without being ruled by the moment.

Self-control is part of spiritual fruit, not merely natural temperament. *"But the fruit of the Spirit is... self-control"* (Galatians 5:22–23, NKJV). That matters not only in private temptation, but also in public conversation.

Respect Opens Doors

You can disagree strongly while still showing respect. Respect says:

- "I hear you."
- "I value you as a person."

Even if: *"I do not agree with your position."*

This keeps the door open.

Respect does not mean surrendering conviction. It means remembering that the person in front of you bears the image of God, even when carrying views you believe are wrong. Once respect disappears, the conversation often becomes less about truth and more about injury. But when respect remains, even disagreement can become meaningful.

This kind of posture makes it easier for truth to remain in the room without poisoning the relationship.

The Danger of Online Behavior

In today's world, many conversations happen online. And unfortunately, this is where many believers:

- Lose their tone
- Lose their patience
- Lose their witness

Behind a screen, it is easier to:

- React quickly
- Speak harshly
- Be careless

But the standard remains the same.

This is especially important in our generation, because distance can make people feel less human to us. The absence of face, voice, and immediate presence often weakens restraint. Believers may type what they would never say in person, and in doing so, they damage their witness while convincing themselves they are defending the truth.

The digital space does not excuse the believer from Christlike speech. It tests it. Every post, reply, comment, and message still carries the responsibility of representation.

Let Your Words Reflect Christ

Before you speak, ask:

- Does this reflect Christ?
- Does this carry truth and grace?
- Will this build or break?

Because you are not just speaking for yourself. You are representing Him.

That question alone can save many conversations. It slows the heart. It checks the motive. It reminds the believer that he is not acting merely as an individual defending a personal opinion. He is carrying the name of Christ into human interaction. That should produce both humility and care.

Sometimes the most spiritual thing you can do is pause long enough to let your spirit come back under the rule of God before you answer.

When to Stay Silent

Sometimes, the most powerful response is silence, or a simple, measured answer. Not every challenge requires:

- A full defense
- A long explanation

Wisdom knows when less is more.

This kind of silence is not fear. It is a restraint. It is the ability to recognize when a conversation is no longer open, when a person is not yet ready, or when saying more would only feed conflict instead of serving truth. Jesus Himself remained silent at certain moments, not because He lacked an answer, but because wisdom governed His response.

A measured answer can carry more weight than a flood of words. Sometimes brevity protects both clarity and peace.

The Power of a Well-Spoken Word

A well-spoken word:

- Lands gently
- Stays longer
- Opens hearts

A harsh word:

- Creates resistance
- Builds walls
- Ends conversations

Well-spoken words do not always sound dramatic, but they often travel farther than we realize. They settle into memory. They leave room for reflection. They continue working after the conversation is over. Harsh words may feel powerful in the moment, but they often produce immediate resistance and lasting distance.

Proverbs 25:11 says, *"A word fitly spoken is like apples of gold in settings of silver"* (NKJV). There is beauty in timely, measured, gracious truth.

A Mature Voice Is Measured

Maturity is not loud. It is:

- Clear
- Calm
- Consistent

And that kind of voice carries influence.

A measured voice does not need theatrics to be strong. It does not need volume to carry authority. It gains influence because people learn that what comes from it is steady, thoughtful, and trustworthy. Over time, consistency in tone becomes part of credibility itself.

This kind of maturity is especially important in difficult spaces. A believer whose voice remains calm and clear under pressure becomes easier to hear, easier to trust, and harder to dismiss.

A Final Reminder

You are not just responsible for what you say. You are responsible for:

- How you say it
- When you say it
- Why do you say it

Because all of it reflects your maturity.

This chapter calls us to more than verbal correctness. It calls us to spiritual alignment in speech. God is not only forming our theology. He is also forming our tone, our reactions, our pace, and our posture. A mature believer learns that content, spirit, and timing all belong together in faithful witness.

Points to Ponder

1. How do I typically respond under pressure?
2. Does my tone reflect Christ in conversations?
3. Am I more focused on being right or being effective?
4. Do I speak with grace as well as truth?
5. Do I become sharper when I feel insecure, challenged, or misunderstood?

1. What does my tone reveal about the present condition of my heart?

2. Where is God inviting me to grow in self-control, patience, and Christlike speech?

Call to Action

This week, focus on your tone in conversations:

- Slow down
- Listen more
- Respond calmly

Let your words carry both:

- Truth
- Grace

Before responding in a difficult moment, take a brief pause and pray inwardly. Ask the Lord to rule your tone before He rules your words through you. Choose one conversation this week where you would normally react quickly, and instead answer with deliberate calmness, respect, and clarity. Afterward, reflect honestly on how that changed the atmosphere.

Declaration

I speak truth with grace and wisdom. My words reflect Christ in every situation. I remain calm, clear, and composed. I do not react, I respond. My voice brings clarity, not confusion. Through me, truth will be heard and received.

I will not use harshness to compensate for insecurity. The Spirit of God is shaping both my message and my manner. My tone, my timing, and my words will reflect the heart of Christ.

Prayer

Father,

Teach me to speak as You would speak. Help me to carry truth with grace and wisdom. Remove every tendency toward harshness or impatience. Give me control over my emotions and clarity in my words. Let my voice reflect Your heart. May every conversation I have bring light and understanding.

Lord, search the places in me where pride, fear, frustration, or insecurity have shaped the way I speak. Purify my spirit so that truth can come through me without distortion. Teach me how to remain firm without becoming harsh, honest without becoming cold, and clear without becoming proud. Let my tone carry peace, my words carry weight, and my presence carry Christ. Make me a believer whose speech opens doors for truth instead of building walls against it. In every conversation, let Your Spirit govern my heart so that what I say, how I say it, and why I say it all bring honor to You.

In Jesus' name,

Amen.

Chapter 13: The Fear Of Being Wrong

Why Insecurity Keeps Christians Silent in Critical Moments

There is a hidden fear that affects more believers than many are willing to admit. It is not always fear of persecution, rejection, or conflict. Sometimes it is the fear of being wrong, the fear of saying something incomplete, the fear of not having the perfect answer, the fear of being exposed in front of people who seem more informed, more articulate, or more confident.

This chapter brings that fear into the light. Not to shame the believer for it, but to help break its power. Because when fear of imperfection rules the heart, faith often becomes quieter than it was ever meant to be.

There is a fear that many believers carry, but rarely name.

It is not always fear of darkness. Not always fear of opposition. Not even fear of rejection. Sometimes, it is simply this: *"What if I say the wrong thing?"* And that fear is powerful enough to make many believers:

- Stay silent
- Avoid conversations
- Withdraw from meaningful engagement

Not because they have no faith, but because they are afraid of imperfection.

This fear often hides beneath respectable language. A believer may say he is waiting for the right moment, trying to be wise, or choosing caution. Sometimes that is true. But other times, the deeper issue is insecurity. He is afraid that if he speaks, his limitations will become visible. He is afraid that if he tries to represent the truth, he may not do it perfectly. And so silence begins to feel safer than obedience.

The Desire to Be Accurate Is Good

Let us begin with balance. Wanting to be accurate is not wrong. It is good. Believers should care about:

- Truth
- Precision
- Faithful representation

That is healthy.

But when the desire for accuracy becomes fear of speaking at all, it has crossed into bondage.

There is a holy difference between reverence and paralysis. Reverence says, *"I want to handle truth well."* Paralysis says, *"If I cannot handle it perfectly, I should say nothing."* One produces humility and growth. The other produces hesitation and absence. The enemy often takes something healthy and pushes it into something restrictive. That is what happens here. A sincere desire to be faithful becomes a fear that keeps the believer from opening his mouth at all.

Perfectionism Is Not Spiritual Maturity

Many believers quietly assume:

- "If I can't answer everything…"
- "I shouldn't say anything."

But that is not maturity. That is perfectionism. And perfectionism often disguises itself as humility.

It sounds humble on the surface. It sounds careful, responsible, and restrained. But often, it is not humility at all. It is self-protection. Humility is willing to speak truthfully while still admitting human limitations. Perfectionism waits for a level of mastery that rarely arrives in real life. As a result, many believers keep postponing obedience until they feel fully ready, and in the process, they miss the very moments God had prepared for their witness.

Truth Can Be Spoken Faithfully Without Being Exhaustively Explained

This is important. You do not need to know everything to say something true. You do not need:

- Complete mastery
- Perfect theological range
- An answer for every objection

to represent Christ meaningfully.

Sometimes, a faithful witness is not comprehensive. It is simply honest and clear.

This truth sets the believer free. God does not require exhaustive brilliance before He can use your voice. Many conversations do not require a full defense of every doctrine. They require one sincere, grounded, truthful response. One clear testimony. One faithful sentence. One thoughtful answer. We often imagine that every moment of witness demands expert-level performance, when in reality, many moments simply call for courage joined with honesty.

In John 9, the man who had been healed by Jesus did not possess a full theological system. Yet he said, *"One thing I know: that though I was blind, now I see"* (John 9:25, NKJV). It was not an exhaustive explanation. But it was true. And truth spoken faithfully still carries power.

Fear of Being Wrong Often Reveals Deeper Issues

Why does this fear become so strong? Because for many believers, being wrong feels personal. It feels like:

- Exposure
- Embarrassment
- Loss of credibility

This reveals something deeper: identity is still too connected to performance.

When identity is not fully settled in Christ, mistakes feel larger than they really are. An imperfect answer feels like a personal failure. A gap in understanding feels like humiliation. A difficult question feels like a threat to worth. But when identity becomes more rooted in God, the believer begins to realize that being incomplete in knowledge does not mean being disqualified in witness. He is not accepted by God because he answers perfectly. He is accepted by God because he belongs to Christ.

The Fear of Mistakes Produces Unnecessary Silence

Let's be honest about the cost. Because of this fear, many believers:

- Miss opportunities to witness
- Avoid important conversations
- Say nothing when truth is needed

Not because they had nothing to offer, but because they feared offering it imperfectly.

This is where the damage becomes real. The issue is not merely internal discomfort. It is of little usefulness. A conversation that could have been meaningful never happened. A searching person never hears the truth that might have helped. A moment of courage dissolves into quiet retreat. And all of it happens not because God withheld grace, but because fear exaggerated the cost of imperfection.

Moses Also Feared Speaking Imperfectly

This struggle is not new. When God called Moses, Moses responded with hesitation: *"Oh my Lord, I am not eloquent..."*, Exodus 4:10

In other words: *"I am not enough for this."*

But God did not accept that excuse. Why? Because the issue was never Moses' perfection. The issue was God's calling.

This is deeply comforting. One of Scripture's great leaders began with the same kind of insecurity many believers still carry. Moses focused on his weakness. God focused on His purpose. Moses saw his limitations. God saw His own sufficiency. This is often the turning point in Christian witness: we stop measuring the moment only by our inadequacy and start seeing it through the faithfulness of the One who sends us.

The Lord asked Moses, *"Who has made man's mouth?"* (Exodus 4:11, NKJV). That question still speaks today. God is not ignorant of your limitations. He calls you with full knowledge of them.

God Does Not Require You to Be Flawless to Be Useful

This must settle deeply in the heart. God uses people who are:

- Growing
- Learning
- Still developing

He does not wait until a believer becomes flawless before allowing them to be useful.

If that were the requirement, no believer would ever be ready. Spiritual usefulness has never been built on flawlessness. It has been built on surrender, growth, faithfulness, and willingness. The Church has often been carried forward by people who were sincere, teachable, available, and dependent on God, even while still growing in many areas.

This does not excuse carelessness. It simply removes the false burden of perfection. The believer must still pursue truth seriously, but he must no longer treat imperfection as proof that he should remain silent.

Being Correctable Is More Important Than Being Impressive

A mature believer is not one who never gets anything wrong. A mature believer is one who:

- Stays teachable
- Receives correction
- Keeps growing

This matters because confidence should not come from pretending to know everything. It should come from being rooted enough to keep learning.

That kind of maturity is beautiful. It does not pretend. It does not posture. It does not collapse when corrected. It remains humble enough to receive truth and strong enough to continue serving. The believer who is teachable is far more useful in the long run than the believer who hides behind silence because he is terrified of ever needing correction.

Proverbs 9:9 says, *"Give instruction to a wise man, and he will be still wiser"* (NKJV). Wisdom is not threatened by growth. Wisdom welcomes it.

You Can Say, "I Don't Know Yet."

One of the healthiest things a believer can learn to say is: *"I don't know the full answer to that yet."*

That is not failure. That is honesty. And honesty builds trust.

Many believers think admitting limitation will weaken their witness. Often, it does the opposite. Honest humility can make a conversation more credible, not less. It tells the other person that your faith is not built on pretense. It shows that your confidence in Christ is strong enough to survive an unanswered question while you continue learning.

A truthful *"I don't know yet"* is better than a forced answer spoken from insecurity. But it should not end there. Mature honesty says, *"I don't know yet, and I am willing to study, pray, and return to this with greater clarity."*

The Enemy Uses Shame to Magnify the Risk

Fear of being wrong is often strengthened by shame. Shame whispers:

- "If you say this imperfectly, they will think you are foolish."
- "If you cannot answer well, you should not speak at all."
- "If you make one mistake, your witness is ruined."

But these are lies.

Shame always exaggerates the consequences of human limitation. It turns normal growth into humiliation. It turns teachability into weakness. It turns one imperfect moment into a false verdict about the whole person. That is not the voice of the Shepherd. God corrects, but He does not crush. He teaches, but He does not shame us into silence.

Courage Is Not the Absence of Incompleteness

Courage does not mean:

- You know everything
- You never hesitate
- You never feel weak

Courage means:

- You speak anyway
- You engage anyway
- You obey anyway

Because truth matters more than your fear.

This is the kind of courage many believers need. Not dramatic confidence, but willing obedience. The courage to speak while still growing. The courage to answer while still learning. The courage to step into the moment, trusting that God can work through sincere faithfulness even when the believer does not feel impressive.

The Holy Spirit Helps in Human Weakness

Never forget this: you do not represent Christ alone. The Holy Spirit helps:

- Guide your words
- Remind you of the truth
- Give wisdom in the moment

This does not remove the need for preparation. But it does remove the burden of self-reliance.

The believer must prepare seriously and depend deeply. Both matter. We study because truth matters. We pray because we know our sufficiency is not in ourselves. The Spirit of God is not merely a comfort after the conversation. He is a helper within it. He can steady the heart, restrain panic, bring Scripture to remembrance, and help a believer say enough, even if not everything.

Jesus said, *"For the Holy Spirit will teach you in that very hour what you ought to say"* (Luke 12:12, NKJV). That promise was never meant to make believers lazy. It was meant to make them dependent.

Practice Removes Some of the Fear

Part of this fear remains strong because many believers have not practiced. So every conversation feels high-pressure. But clarity grows through use.

The more you:

- Think
- Speak
- Engage

The more confidence develops.

This is simple but important. Many things that feel terrifying at first become more manageable through faithful practice. The first time a believer answers a difficult question, it may feel awkward. The second time, less so. Over time, what once felt overwhelming begins to feel navigable. Confidence is often built not only through knowledge but through repeated obedience.

Silence Does Not Protect You as Much as You Think

Many believers stay silent to avoid the risk of being wrong. But silence carries its own cost. Silence can:

- Confirm assumptions
- Missed divine opportunities
- Leave searching hearts unanswered

So the question is not only, *"What if I speak imperfectly?"* It is also, *"What is lost if I say nothing?"*

That question deserves to linger. We often overestimate the danger of an imperfect answer while underestimating the cost of no answer at all. An imperfect witness can still open a door. Silence often leaves the door closed. A sincere response may still plant a seed. Silence often leaves the ground untouched.

Faithful Representation Is Often Simpler Than We Imagine

Sometimes the believer imagines that a witness must sound polished. But often, the most meaningful responses are:

- Simple
- Sincere
- Grounded
- Human

Not:

- Theatrical
- Academic
- Forced

Just real.

This matters especially for believers who become intimidated by people who sound highly educated, highly skeptical, or highly articulate. You do not need to become artificial to be faithful. The goal is not performance. The goal is honest representation. Many people are moved not by polished speech, but by words that feel clean, thoughtful, and real.

From Fear of Being Wrong to Willingness to Grow

The shift must be this:

From:

- "I must never be wrong."

to:

- "I am willing to grow while being faithful."

That is freedom. That is maturity. That is usable faith.

This shift breaks a hidden chain in many believers. Once you stop demanding perfection from yourself before obedience, you become far more available to God. You remain serious about truth, but you no longer worship flawless performance. You become willing to learn publicly, grow steadily, and represent Christ sincerely.

A Final Encouragement

You may not always say everything perfectly. But if your heart is sincere, your spirit is humble, and your words are truthful, God can still use you powerfully.

Do not let the fear of imperfection rob the world of the witness God placed in you. Learn. Study. Grow. Be teachable. But do not hide. The One who called you already knows you are still being formed. He did not wait for perfection before giving you purpose.

Points to Ponder

1. Do I stay silent because I fear being wrong?
2. Have I confused humility with perfectionism?
3. Do mistakes feel too personal to me?
4. Am I more committed to looking prepared or to being faithful?
5. What opportunities have I missed because I demanded too much perfection from myself before speaking?
6. How does my fear of imperfection reveal areas where my identity may still be tied to performance?
7. What would change if I truly believed God could use me while I am still growing?

Call to Action

This week, when a faith conversation opens, do not wait for the perfect answer. Offer one honest, clear response. If needed, say: *"This is what I know,"* or *"I'm still growing in that, but here is what I can say clearly."*

Then take note afterward. Reflect on what went well, what felt weak, and what you want to understand better next time. Let the conversation become part of your growth instead of a source of shame. Practice faithfulness, not perfection.

Declaration

I do not fear being imperfect. I am growing, learning, and becoming stronger in truth. God can use me even while I am still developing. I speak with humility, honesty, and courage. I will not let fear silence my witness. Through Christ, I will grow in clarity and confidence.

I reject the lie that I must be flawless before I can be useful. My identity is rooted in Christ, not in perfect performance. I will obey God with a teachable spirit, a sincere heart, and a willing voice.

Prayer

Father,

Deliver me from the fear of being wrong. Free me from the pressure of trying to be perfect before I speak. Teach me to handle truth with humility and faithfulness. Give me the courage to speak, even while I am still growing. Help me to be teachable, honest, and steady. Let my confidence rest in You, not in flawless performance. Use my voice for Your glory, and keep shaping me as I serve You.

Lord, heal every place in me where shame has made silence feel safer than obedience. Break the fear that tells me I must know everything before I can say anything. Teach me to trust You in my weakness, to remain humble in my learning, and to stay available in every moment You open. Let my mistakes not drive me into hiding, but into deeper growth. Give me a calm heart, a teachable mind, and a courageous spirit. And when I speak, let my words be sincere, clear, and faithful enough for You to use.

In Jesus' name,

Amen.

Chapter 14: The Church As An Echo Chamber

Why Constant Agreement Can Make Christians Socially Fragile

There is a danger that does not always look dangerous at first. It can feel comforting, affirming, even spiritually healthy on the surface. It is the danger of living in circles where our beliefs are rarely questioned, our language is always understood, and our convictions are constantly reinforced without ever being tested in real life.

This chapter is not attacking the Christian community, because godly fellowship is a gift. But it is exposing what happens when community becomes containment, when agreement replaces growth, and when the Church becomes a place where believers are encouraged yet never prepared.

There is a hidden weakness growing in many Christian communities. It is not false doctrine. It is not open rebellion. It is not a lack of passion. It is overexposure to agreement.

Many believers spend most of their lives in environments where:

- Everyone thinks alike
- Everyone speaks the same language
- Everyone reinforces the same convictions

And while this may feel spiritually safe, it can quietly make them socially fragile.

That fragility often goes unnoticed until the believer steps outside the protected circle. Inside the echo of agreement, confidence feels strong because nothing is pressing against it. But once that same believer enters a setting where his convictions are questioned, misunderstood, or challenged, he may discover that what felt like strength was never fully tested. This is why the issue is not the fellowship itself. The issue is what happens when fellowship becomes the only environment in which faith knows how to function.

Agreement Is Not the Same as Maturity

Let us say this clearly. Being surrounded by people who agree with you does not automatically make you strong. It may make you:

- Comfortable
- Affirmed
- Emotionally supported

But it does not necessarily make you:

- Clear
- Prepared
- Resilient

Maturity requires more than reinforcement. It requires formation. A believer can become fluent in the language of his own circle and still remain unprepared for the real demands of witness. He may know how to sound strong where no resistance exists, yet not know how to stay steady where resistance appears. This is one of the quiet differences between supported faith and tested faith. Both matter, but they are not the same.

The Function of Christian Community

A Christian community is necessary. It is a place for:

- Encouragement
- Worship

- Discipleship
- Mutual strengthening

That is biblical.

Scripture never treats fellowship as optional. The body of Christ is one of God's great gifts to the believer. We need one another for prayer, correction, comfort, growth, and shared devotion. A healthy community can strengthen identity, deepen understanding, and restore weary hearts. So this chapter is not arguing against the Church gathering, loving, and building one another up.

Hebrews 10:24–25 reminds us not to forsake assembling together, but to encourage one another (NKJV). Fellowship matters deeply. The problem begins only when fellowship becomes the whole environment of our faith instead of a place from which faith is strengthened and then sent outward.

When Community Becomes Containment

The problem begins when the community stops being a place of preparation and becomes a place of containment.

When believers only:

- Talk to each other

- Learn from each other

- Affirm each other

And rarely engage beyond that, they begin to confuse shared reinforcement with real readiness.

Containment happens quietly. The Church still meets, still sings, still studies, still serves, still speaks of truth. But slowly, the believer's faith becomes shaped almost entirely by environments where it is never stretched by real-world resistance. Eventually, even a simple disagreement can start to feel threatening, not because the truth is weak, but because the believer has lived too long without having to carry it outside familiar walls.

The Echo Chamber Effect

An echo chamber does something subtle. It repeats your own beliefs back to you so often that you begin to assume:

- Everyone should understand them easily
- No serious questions remain
- Anyone who disagrees is simply blind or rebellious

This produces believers who are:

- Certain without depth
- Confident without understanding
- Strong in familiar language but weak in unfamiliar spaces

This is dangerous because it gives the appearance of stability without always producing the substance of maturity. Repetition can strengthen truth, but it can also create the illusion that understanding has become deeper than it actually is. A believer may hear the same ideas echoed so often that he mistakes familiarity for mastery. Then, when a thoughtful question arises from someone outside that circle, he discovers that he has repeated much more than he has processed.

Why Social Fragility Develops

Believers become socially fragile when they are rarely exposed to:

- Different worldviews
- Honest objections
- Challenging questions

- Unfamiliar language

So when they finally encounter them, they feel:

- Threatened
- Overwhelmed
- Defensive
- Or silent

This fragility is not always emotional weakness. Sometimes it is simply a lack of training. A believer who has never learned to engage differences with patience and clarity will often feel unstable the first time he must do so. He may not know how to translate what he believes into language a nonbeliever can understand. He may not know how to stay calm when assumptions are challenged. He may not know how to separate the discomfort of disagreement from actual danger. These are signs that formation has remained too sheltered.

Jesus Did Not Build an Echo Chamber

Jesus taught His disciples in private. But he also took them into:

- Crowds
- Conflict
- Public questions
- Opposing environments

He did not prepare them only through agreement. He prepared them through exposure, instruction, and engagement.

This is an important part of His method. Jesus gave His disciples intimacy, but not insulation. He explained the truth to them, but He also let them watch the truth function in complicated settings. They saw Him answer critics, touch broken people, correct religious blindness, and remain steady in public tension. In other words, He did not train them only in protected devotion. He trained them in a live mission.

That pattern still matters. The Church must be a place where believers are not only comforted, but equipped for the world they will actually face.

The Danger of Untested Language

Many believers know how to say things like:

- "I'm covered by grace."
- "God is good."
- "I walk by faith."

These are true and precious statements. But when pressed with real questions, many cannot explain what those phrases actually mean.

Why? Because repeated language is not the same as internalized understanding.

This is where echo chambers often create shallow fluency. A believer becomes comfortable repeating familiar truths but may never have slowed down long enough to wrestle with their meaning, their depth, or their application in conversation with people who do not already share the same assumptions. Phrases that sound powerful inside Christian settings may sound vague outside them if the believer has not learned how to unfold them clearly.

God is not calling us to abandon the language of faith. He is calling us to inhabit it deeply enough that we can carry its meaning into real human conversation.

A Faith That Has Never Been Stretched Stays Weak

Just as muscles grow through resistance, conviction often grows through challenge. If your faith is never:

- Questioned
- Examined
- Required to explain itself

Then parts of it may remain underdeveloped.

This is not because questioning is greater than truth. It is because resistance often reveals what reinforcement hides. A believer may feel very secure in what he has inherited until he is asked to explain it with thought and grace. At that moment, weak spots appear, not to shame him, but to show him where growth is needed.

James 1:3 says that the testing of your faith produces patience (NKJV). While that verse has a wider meaning, the principle still helps us here: tested faith often becomes stronger faith.

Why the Church Must Be More Than a Comfort Zone

The Church should comfort believers. But it must not only comfort them. It must also:

- Train them
- Stretch them
- Prepare them
- Send them

Because if the Church becomes only a place of refuge, it may fail as a place of formation.

A church that only soothes without strengthening can unintentionally produce dependence on safety rather than readiness for mission. People leave feeling encouraged, but not always equipped. They know how to receive truth in familiar conditions, but not always how to represent it when familiarity disappears. The goal is not to make church harsher. The goal is to make it more complete.

Healthy Fellowship Should Produce Courage, Not Dependence

Christian fellowship should do something beautiful: it should strengthen you enough to leave the room more ready for the world. Not more afraid of it. Not more detached from it. Not more dependent on constant affirmation from your own circle.

That is one of the marks of a healthy community. It does not make believers smaller. It sends them out stronger. It gives them language, understanding, prayer, and identity that can remain steady in public life. If our gatherings only make us feel safe among ourselves, but not useful among others, then something about our formation is incomplete.

The Difference between Fellowship and Insulation

Fellowship says: *"We strengthen one another in Christ."* Insulation says, *"We remain here because outside is too uncomfortable."*

Fellowship produces growth. Insulation produces fragility.

This difference is vital. Fellowship is a gift of God. Insulation is often a misuse of that gift. One builds up the believer and prepares him for obedience. The other keeps him tucked away from the very places where obedience must become visible. One leads to readiness. The other leads to dependency on controlled environments.

How Echo Chambers Distort Perception

When believers live only in agreement, they can begin to develop distorted expectations. They may assume:

- Truth should always be immediately welcomed
- People who disagree are simply hostile
- Complex questions are signs of rebellion

This makes real-world engagement harder.

It becomes harder because the believer has not been trained to expect complexity with patience. He may walk into a conversation already irritated by the fact that someone does not understand what seems obvious inside his own circle. But outside the echo chamber, language is different, assumptions are different, wounds are different, and the path to understanding is often slower. The believer must be prepared for that.

Social Strength Requires Exposure with Formation

The answer is not reckless exposure. The answer is wise engagement with strong formation. Believers need:

- Sound teaching
- Deep identity
- Biblical clarity
- Real interaction with people who think differently

This builds resilience.

In other words, the solution is balance. We do not throw believers into confusion without grounding. But neither do we keep them so protected that they never learn how to stand. True formation gives the believer roots and then teaches him how to remain rooted while the winds are blowing. That is how resilience grows.

Paul Did Not Stay Only in Safe Rooms

Paul reasoned in synagogues, spoke in marketplaces, stood before rulers, and engaged philosophers in Athens.

He did not keep the truth only inside affirming spaces. He carried it into public tension.

Acts 17 shows this vividly. Paul encountered a city full of idols and conflicting ideas, yet he did not retreat from conversation. He entered it thoughtfully. He observed carefully. He spoke with courage and intelligence. This was not a compromise. It was a mature engagement.

The early Church did not grow by staying inside protected circles alone. It moved outward with truth that had become alive enough to enter difficult environments.

The Church Must Recover Conversational Strength

Many believers know how to preach to people. Fewer know how to speak with people. That is part of the problem.

Echo chambers train proclamation in safe spaces, but not always dialogue in real spaces.

Conversational strength is different from sermon strength. It requires listening, translating, patience, emotional steadiness, and the ability to stay human while remaining clear. A believer may sound powerful in front of those who already agree, yet feel lost in ordinary one-on-one conversations where truth must be carried gently and thoughtfully. The Church must help believers grow there, too.

The Goal Is Not Less Fellowship, But Better Formation

Let this be clear. The answer is not less Church. Not less fellowship. Not less shared conviction. The answer is:

- Fellowship that strengthens believers for engagement
- Teaching that prepares believers for questions
- Community that builds resilience, not dependency

We do not need weaker churches. We need stronger ones. Churches where believers are loved deeply and prepared honestly. Churches where questions are not feared. Churches where people are taught not only what to believe, but how to carry belief into a complicated world with grace and steadiness.

A Healthy Church Sends People Back into the World Stronger

A healthy church gathering should leave the believer saying, *"I am more ready now."* Not, *"I never want to leave this safe environment."* Because the purpose of spiritual strengthening is not permanent retreat, it is faithful return.

This is the rhythm of the Kingdom. We gather, we are strengthened, we are clarified, we are corrected, we are nourished, and then we are sent again. A church that forgets the sending part may still be comforting, but it is no longer fully functioning.

A Final Confrontation

If your faith only feels strong when you are surrounded by agreement, then it is not yet as strong as it needs to be. That is not a condemnation. It is an invitation.

It is an invitation to grow beyond borrowed confidence and into deeper stability. It is an invitation to let truth become rooted enough in you that it can live outside the echo of your own circle. It is an invitation to become the kind of believer who can remain loving, clear, and present even when agreement disappears.

Points to Ponder

1. Do I spend most of my spiritual life only around people who already agree with me?
2. Has constant affirmation made me less prepared for real-world engagement?
3. Am I strong in Christian language but weak in everyday conversation?
4. Does my community prepare me for the world, or mainly protect me from it?
5. Have I mistaken repeated agreement for actual maturity?
6. What happens to me when I step outside familiar Christian spaces and encounter real disagreement?
7. In what ways might God be calling me to grow from supported faith into tested, resilient faith?

Call to Action

This week, intentionally step beyond your usual circle. Have one real conversation with someone who thinks differently. Do not go to argue. Go to:

- Listen

- Understand
- Practice carrying truth outside the echo chamber

Afterward, reflect honestly. What felt difficult? What exposed weakness? What surprised you? Let that moment become training. Then return to Scripture and prayer, not to hide again, but to grow stronger for the next conversation.

Declaration

My faith is not dependent on constant agreement. I am being strengthened for real-world engagement. I grow in clarity, resilience, and understanding. I will not live only inside safe echoes. I am called to carry truth with courage into the world. Through Christ, my faith will become strong, steady, and useful.

I reject the comfort that weakens my witness. God is forming in me a faith that can remain clear outside familiar circles. I am strengthened in fellowship, but I am sent on a mission.

Prayer

Father,

Thank You for the gift of Christian community. Thank You for fellowship, encouragement, and shared faith. But do not let me become dependent on agreement in a way that weakens my witness. Strengthen me beyond comfort. Teach me how to carry truth outside familiar spaces.

Give me resilience, clarity, and courage. Make my faith strong enough to stand in real conversations and real environments. Let the community that builds me also prepare me. And let my life reflect a faith that is not sheltered into weakness, but strengthened for assignment.

Lord, expose every place in me where comfort has quietly replaced growth. Show me where I have hidden inside familiar language and familiar people instead of allowing my faith to become stronger through real engagement. Teach me to receive the gift of fellowship without using it as insulation from the world You have called me to reach. Make me thoughtful, grounded, and steady. Let my confidence come from truth deeply formed in me, not merely from being surrounded by people who repeat what I already know. Build in me a faith that can listen without fear, speak without panic, and remain faithful when agreement is no longer around me.

In Jesus' name,

Amen.

Chapter 15: Faith That Enters Systems

Why Kingdom Influence Must Move Beyond Individuals into Structures

This chapter widens the believer's sense of assignment. Many Christians understand personal witness, private holiness, and one-on-one impact, but become uncertain when faith must move into larger environments that shape communities, policies, learning, opportunity, and culture. Yet the Kingdom of God does not stop at the boundary of the individual soul. It reaches people, and through transformed people, it reaches structures.

This chapter invites the believer to stop seeing systems as places to fear and start seeing them as places where truth, integrity, wisdom, and excellence are desperately needed.

Many believers are comfortable with:

- Personal faith
- Private morality
- Individual impact

But they hesitate when it comes to:

- Systems
- Structures
- Institutions

And yet systems are what shape:

- Culture
- Economics
- Education

- Values at scale

So if believers stay out of systems, they surrender influence.

That surrender is often quiet. It does not always look like rebellion or indifference. Sometimes it looks like caution. Sometimes it looks like a narrow definition of spirituality. Sometimes it sounds humble, as though faith should stay in the realm of the personal and leave larger structures untouched. But when believers withdraw from systems entirely, they leave those systems to be shaped by values that may be far from the heart of God.

What Are Systems?

Systems are organized structures that influence how people live. For example:

- Business systems, economics, trade, and employment
- Government systems, laws, policies
- Educational systems, what people learn
- Media systems, what people see and believe

These systems:

- Shape thinking
- Direct behavior
- Influence entire communities

This is why systems cannot be treated as distant or irrelevant. They are not abstract ideas floating far above daily life. They affect what people can access, what they are taught, what is rewarded, what is normalized, what is protected, and what is neglected. In many cases, people live under the influence of systems long before they ever stop to examine them.

Why Systems Matter

You can change individuals, but systems affect multitudes. One transformed person helps a few. A transformed system impacts thousands.

This is why influence must expand.

The Kingdom always values the individual, but it does not stop there. A believer who helps one life matters deeply. But when believers also bring righteousness, wisdom, and integrity into the systems that shape many lives, the reach of that faith grows wider. This is not replacing personal ministry. It is extending it.

Proverbs 11:11 says, *"By the blessing of the upright the city is exalted"* (NKJV). That verse carries a larger vision than private morality alone. It suggests that the presence and conduct of the righteous can affect whole communities.

Jesus Engaged Systems, Not Just Individuals

Jesus:

- Challenged religious systems
- Exposed corrupt leadership
- Addressed economic injustice
- Spoke into power structures

He did not ignore systems. He confronted them with the truth.

This is important because some believers imagine Jesus only as one who dealt with private sin in private hearts. But the Gospels show something broader. He also confronted structures of hypocrisy, exploitation, and distorted authority. His ministry was deeply personal, but never merely private.

When Jesus cleansed the temple, He was not only correcting a few individuals. He was confronting a system that had turned sacred space into a place of exploitation. *"My house shall be called a house of prayer, but you have made it a 'den of thieves'"* (Matthew 21:13, NKJV). That moment shows us that truth sometimes must speak not only to personal conduct, but to institutional corruption.

The Mistake of Avoidance

Some believers say, *"I just focus on people, not systems."* But this creates a limitation. Because while you help individuals, systems may continue to:

- Oppress
- Mislead
- Corrupt

And those same individuals remain affected.

There is compassion in helping individuals, and that should never be minimized. But if the structures around those individuals remain broken, the pressure against human flourishing continues. This is why Kingdom thinking must mature. It must care for people personally while also asking larger questions about the environments shaping their lives.

You Were Not Called Only to Survive Systems

Many believers operate with this mindset: *"How do I stay clean in a broken system?"* That is good, but incomplete.

The higher question is: *"How do I bring change within the system I am part of?"*

That is a meaningful shift. Survival asks how to avoid being damaged. The assignment asks how to become useful. Survival focuses mainly on protection. The assignment also includes a contribution. The believer is right to desire purity, but purity alone is not the full picture. God also calls us to carry His wisdom and character into the places where we live and work.

Joseph: A Model of System Influence

Joseph did not avoid Egypt. He entered its system, rose within it, and influenced it.

And through his position:

- A nation was preserved
- A famine was managed
- Resources were distributed

That is systemic impact.

Joseph's life is one of Scripture's clearest examples of righteous influence within a complex structure. He did not begin with power, status, or control. He began with faithfulness in difficulty. Yet over time, God positioned him where wisdom could preserve many lives. That story reminds the believer that systems are not outside the reach of divine purpose.

Genesis 41 shows Joseph moving from prison into administrative influence, and the effect was far greater than personal advancement. It became a preservation for many. This is one of the holy possibilities of Kingdom competence: God can place a believer where wisdom becomes protection and provision for others.

Daniel: Influence without Compromise

Daniel worked in:

- A pagan government
- A foreign system

Yet:

- He remained faithful
- He did not compromise
- He influenced leadership

This is the balance: presence without compromise, influence without loss of identity.

Daniel is especially important because he shows that participation in a secular or ungodly environment does not automatically require surrender of godliness. He remained distinct in conviction while still being useful in governance. He did not disappear. He did not blend in. He lived with a rare combination of excellence, discipline, prayer, and courage.

Daniel 6:3 says, *"Then this Daniel distinguished himself above the governors and satraps, because an excellent spirit was in him"* (NKJV). That phrase is powerful. His distinction was not noise. It was substance. An excellent spirit made him visible.

Why Many Believers Stay Out

Because systems can feel:

- Complex
- Corrupt
- Intimidating

And some believe: *"If I enter, I will be compromised."*

But the issue is not the system. It is the strength of the believer within it.

This is where spiritual formation matters. A weak identity fears every difficult environment as though it will automatically swallow conviction. But a rooted believer learns how to stay clear inside complicated places. The answer is not naïve exposure or careless ambition. The answer is deeper strength in Christ, stronger convictions, and greater maturity.

Systems Do Not Change Themselves

If people of integrity avoid systems, then systems will be shaped by those without integrity. And that is exactly what we see in many places today.

This is one of the sobering realities of public life. Vacuums do not remain empty. If believers with wisdom, character, and humility refuse to enter important spaces, those spaces will still be filled, but not necessarily by those who carry justice, truth, or moral steadiness. Absence has consequences.

The Call to Competence

To influence systems, you must develop:

- Skill
- Knowledge
- Excellence

Because influence is not given. It is earned through:

- Competence
- Consistency
- Credibility

This chapter is important because it does not allow believers to confuse good intentions with meaningful readiness. Systems are often shaped by those who understand how they function. That means faith must be joined to development. The believer must grow not only in prayer, but also in skill; not only in devotion, but also in discipline; not only in conviction, but also in competence.

Colossians 3:23 gives a principle that applies here beautifully: *"And whatever you do, do it heartily, as to the Lord and not to men"* (NKJV). Excellence is not vanity when it is offered to God. It becomes part of the witness.

Spiritual without Excellence Is Ineffective

Some believers rely only on:

- Spiritual language
- Good intentions

But lack:

- Professional competence
- Practical understanding

And this limits their influence.

Because systems respond to:

- Results
- Performance
- Value

This is not a call to become worldly. It is a call to become effective. Spiritual passion is precious, but if it is never developed into trustworthy execution, many doors of influence remain closed. A believer in a workplace, classroom, institution, or civic setting must learn how to embody both godliness and usefulness.

Faith Must Be Carried into Function

It is not enough to pray. You must also:

- Perform
- Produce
- Contribute

with excellence.

Prayer remains essential, but prayer was never meant to excuse neglect. God is glorified not only when the believer seeks Him privately, but also when that inner life produces faithful work, wise contribution, and reliable stewardship in visible spaces. This is where many Christians need a broader understanding of witness.

Integrity Within Systems

When you enter systems:

- Do not adopt corruption
- Do not justify compromise
- Do not lose conviction

Instead:

- Stand firm
- Act wisely
- Lead by example

This is the tension of faithful influence. The believer enters systems not to be absorbed by them, but to remain whole within them. He must resist the temptation to excuse small compromises in the name of effectiveness. Real Kingdom influence loses its beauty the moment integrity is traded for access.

"He who walks with integrity walks securely" (Proverbs 10:9, NKJV). Integrity may not always create the fastest rise, but it creates the strongest foundation.

Influence Begins Where You Are

You do not need a high position to begin influencing.

Wherever you are:

- Your workplace
- Your organization
- Your community

You can:

- Bring integrity
- Introduce wisdom
- Model excellence

This protects the believer from waiting for a title before becoming useful. Influence is not only for those at the top. It begins in daily conduct, dependable work, wise choices, fair treatment of others, thoughtful leadership in small responsibilities, and courage in moments that seem ordinary. God often builds a larger influence through smaller faithfulness.

Small Influence Leads to Greater Opportunity

Faithfulness in small areas:

- Builds trust
- Opens doors
- Expands influence

This is how Joseph and Daniel rose.

The Kingdom pattern is often gradual. God does not always begin with visibility. He often begins with stewardship. He watches how a person handles what is small, unseen, or limited. Over time, credibility grows. Trust deepens. Doors open. This means small responsibilities should never be despised by the believer who desires greater impact.

Jesus said, *"He who is faithful in what is least is faithful also in much"* (Luke 16:10, NKJV). That principle reaches directly into the message of this chapter

The Fear of Visibility

Influencing systems often means:

- Being seen
- Being evaluated
- Being challenged

And that can be uncomfortable. But influence requires:

- Visibility
- Responsibility
- Courage

Some believers are not only afraid of corruption. They are afraid of exposure. To influence systems is to become visible enough to be tested, discussed, and sometimes opposed. That can feel costly. But hidden faith cannot fully shape public environments. Courage is needed not only to stay pure, but also to stay present when visibility increases.

A Shift in Mindset

Move from:

- *"I just need to stay right."*

to:

- *"I am here to make a difference."*

That does not reduce holiness. It deepens the assignment. The believer stops measuring faithfulness only by personal preservation and begins to ask how God might use his presence to strengthen what is weak, correct what is crooked, and improve what affects others.

The Responsibility of Kingdom Carriers

You carry:

- Values
- Truth
- Perspective

that systems need, not to control, but to:

- Bring alignment
- Introduce integrity
- Create balance

This is a very important distinction. Kingdom influence is not about domination, ego, or the hunger to control institutions for personal power. It is about stewardship. It is about carrying God's wisdom in ways that serve people, restrain corruption, support what is just, and make environments more truthful and humane.

A Warning

If believers remain absent, then systems will:

- Drift further
- Become more broken
- Impact more people negatively

Silence and absence have consequences.

This warning should be received with seriousness. It is not enough to criticize the state of institutions from a distance while refusing the burden of participation. Broken systems often remain broken because too few people of conviction are willing to stay in the room long enough to serve faithfully and persist wisely.

A Call to Rise

The time for:

- Passive Christianity
- Private faith
- Limited engagement

It's over.

Believers must:

- Step in
- Stand firm
- Bring influence

This call is not to restless activism for its own sake. It is a call to mature obedience. The world does not merely need Christians who speak about values. It needs believers who embody them in structures that shape many lives.

A Final Perspective

You are not just a participant. You are a representative. Wherever you are placed, you carry responsibility.

That is the dignity of this chapter. The believer is not an accidental presence in his field, organization, profession, or community. He is there with the possibility of representation. God may use his words, decisions, standards, work ethic, wisdom, and consistency to touch far more than he can presently see.

Points to Ponder

1. What systems am I currently part of?
2. Am I influencing them, or just existing within them?
3. Where do I need to grow in competence and excellence?
4. Am I avoiding opportunities to influence?
5. Do I secretly believe that faith belongs only in private life and not in structures that shape society?

1. Where has fear of complexity, corruption, or visibility kept me from embracing a larger assignment?

2. What kind of witness would it become if my integrity and competence matured together in the system where God has placed me?

Call to Action

Identify one system you are part of:

- Workplace
- Organization
- Community

Ask: *"How can I bring value, integrity, and influence here?"* Then take one intentional step.

Make that step practical and specific. It may be improving your work, addressing a recurring problem with wisdom, strengthening fairness in one area, becoming more excellent in your role, or showing unusual integrity where compromise has become normal. Do not wait for a larger platform. Begin where your feet already stand.

Declaration

I am called to influence, not just exist. I bring integrity, excellence, and wisdom into every system I enter. I do not compromise; I stand firm. God has positioned me for impact. Through me, systems will be touched and transformed. I am a carrier of Kingdom influence.

I will not retreat from structures that shape lives when God is calling me to serve within them. The Lord is developing both my character and my competence for meaningful assignments. Wherever He places me, I will bring truth, steadiness, wisdom, and faithful presence.

Prayer

Father,

Thank you for placing me where I am. Help me see my environment as an assignment. Give me the wisdom, skill, and excellence needed to influence systems. Strengthen me to stand firm without compromise. Open doors for greater impact. Let my life bring alignment, integrity, and transformation.

Lord, deliver me from every small view of faith that keeps me content with private conviction while larger environments remain untouched. Teach me how to carry Your heart into the systems around me with humility, maturity, and courage. Deepen my character so that influence does not corrupt me. Strengthen my competence so sincerity does not remain ineffective. Help me to honor You not only in prayer and worship, but also in work, leadership, responsibility, and public faithfulness. Let the places I enter become better because Your wisdom, truth, and integrity are at work through me.

In Jesus' name,
Amen.

Chapter 16: From Avoidance To Influence

The Shift Every Believer Must Make

There comes a sacred moment in the life of a believer when knowledge can no longer remain admired from a distance. What we have learned begins to ask something of us. Truth moves from being something we agree with to something we must embody. This chapter stands in that moment. It is not merely about learning more, but about crossing a threshold, where conviction becomes movement, and where the light God placed within us begins to step into places that once felt easier to avoid.

There comes a point where knowledge is no longer enough.

You have:

- Understood identity
- Seen the model of Jesus
- Gained clarity in belief
- Learned how to engage
- Seen the call to impact money, justice, and systems

Now the question is no longer, "Do I understand?" The question is, "What will I do with what I now know?"

This is one of the most important transitions in the Christian life. A believer can spend years gathering insight, hearing truth, recognizing patterns, and even agreeing with all that God is saying, yet still remain strangely inactive. But revelation was never meant to end in recognition alone. It was meant to produce a response. When God gives understanding, He is not only informing the mind. He is awakening responsibility in the heart.

The Era of Passive Christianity Must End

For too long, many believers have lived in:

- Comfort
- Safety
- Routine

Faith has been:

- Practiced privately
- Expressed selectively
- Protected carefully

But not:

- Lived boldly
- Expressed clearly
- Applied consistently

And that must change.

There is a quiet sorrow in this kind of passivity. Not because the believer has stopped loving God, but because love has not yet become full obedience in public life. Too much of modern faith has remained contained, sincere but restrained; alive, but hesitant; convinced, but rarely visible where it matters most. Yet the hour we are in demands more than private devotion alone. It requires a believer who is willing to carry truth beyond comfort and into responsibility.

James 1:22 gives a needed warning here: "But be doers of the word, and not hearers only, deceiving yourselves" (NKJV). Hearing is not the end of spiritual maturity. Response is.

Avoidance Has a Cost

Avoidance may feel safe. But it produces:

- Lost opportunities
- Missed impact
- Silent influence

Every time you:

- Stay quiet when you should speak
- Withdraw when you should engage
- Hold back when you should act

something is lost.

Not just for you, but for those around you.

This is why avoidance can never be treated as harmless. It is rarely neutral. Each missed moment may look small by itself, yet over time, those moments form a pattern. A searching person remains unanswered. A needed word remains unspoken. A place that could have been touched by truth remains unchanged. Fear often makes withdrawal look like protection, but in reality, it can become a quiet form of disobedience that costs far more than we first realize.

Influence Is Not Automatic

Being a believer does not automatically make you influential. Influence requires:

- Intentionality
- Presence
- Action

You must choose it.

This is a necessary correction. Salvation gives identity, but influence requires participation. A believer may carry truth within and still fail to affect the world around him if he never allows that truth to become visible through choice, conduct, and courageous presence. Influence is not magic. It is stewardship. It grows where believers decide that what God has placed in them must no longer remain hidden.

The Shift Begins in the Mind

Before your actions change, your mindset must change:

- From: *"I want to stay safe."*
  To: *"I am called to make an impact."*
- From: *"I hope I'm not challenged."*
  To: *"I am ready when I am."*
- From: *"I'll stay in my lane."*
  To: *"I will step into my assignment."*

Every outward shift begins with an inward permission. The mind must first stop interpreting challenge as an interruption and begin seeing it as part of the calling. Many believers remain stuck, not because they lack sincerity, but because their internal posture still leans toward self-protection. Once the mind begins to agree with God's purpose, the life gradually follows. The believer starts reading situations differently. What once looked like an inconvenience begins to look like an assignment.

Romans 12:2 reminds us, "Be transformed by the renewing of your mind" (NKJV). Renewal is not abstract. It changes how we see ourselves, how we see our surroundings, and what we believe obedience should look like in real life.

You Were Never Called to Blend In

Let this be clear: you were not called to fit into culture. You were called to influence it.

Blending in removes distinction. And without distinction, there is no influence.

This distinction is not about arrogance or performance. It is about clarity. If the believer becomes so softened by the environment that nothing meaningfully different remains visible, then the witness weakens. Light influences because it does not become darkness. Salt preserves because it does not lose its substance. The believer must never confuse acceptance with fruitfulness. What makes a life useful to God is not how completely it disappears into the atmosphere around it, but how faithfully it carries another Kingdom within that atmosphere.

Every Environment Is an Opportunity

Start seeing differently. Your workplace is not just a job. Your conversations are not random. Your relationships are not accidental. They are all:

- Opportunities
- Platforms
- Assignments

This is where ordinary life begins to look holy again. The believer no longer divides existence into "spiritual moments" and "everything else." He begins to understand that God often works through what appears routine. A meeting, a lunch, a difficult conversation, a recurring relationship, a neighborhood interaction, a moment of pressure, each of these may carry more purpose than we realize when our eyes are open to assignment.

As Esther 4:14 reminds us, "Yet who knows whether you have come to the kingdom for such a time as this?" (NKJV). Even placement can carry purpose when God is involved.

Small Acts Create Large Impact

Influence does not always start big. It starts with:

- One conversation
- One decision
- One act of courage

And those small moments:

- Build confidence
- Expand reach
- Create momentum

Many believers delay obedience because they imagine influence must begin with something dramatic. But God often begins with what feels simple. A faithful answer. A truthful choice. A compassionate response. A refusal to withdraw. These moments may seem small in the beginning, yet they train the soul. They build courage where fear once ruled. They teach the believer that obedience does not need spectacle to carry power.

Consistency Builds Credibility

Influence is not built in one moment. It is built over time through:

- Consistency
- Integrity
- Reliability

People watch:

- How you live
- How you respond
- How you handle pressure

And over time, trust is formed.

There is a quiet strength in a life that remains steady over time. People may not always respond to a single statement, but they often remember repeated evidence of character. They remember the believer who remained calm when others panicked, honest when compromise was easier, kind when harshness was normal, and clear when confusion was spreading. Credibility grows slowly, but it gives weight to truth when the moment to speak finally comes.

"He who is faithful in what is least is faithful also in much" (Luke 16:10, NKJV). Faithfulness in ordinary moments is often the soil from which meaningful influence grows.

Courage Is Required

Let's not pretend. Influence requires courage, the courage to:

- Speak when it is uncomfortable
- Stand when it is unpopular
- Act when it is inconvenient

Without courage:

- Knowledge stays inactive
- Potential stays unrealized

This is where many believers quietly hesitate. They know what is true, but courage becomes the bridge they have not yet crossed. Yet courage is not the absence of trembling. It is the willingness to obey while still feeling the weight of the moment. Many of the most meaningful acts of faith are not loud. They are simply brave enough to move when silence would have felt easier.

"Be strong and of good courage; do not be afraid" (Joshua 1:9, NKJV). God has always known that obedience often requires courage, and He has always supplied His presence with that command.

You Will Not Always Be Accepted

Let's be honest. Not everyone will agree. Not everyone will accept. Not everyone will respond positively. But that is not the goal.

The goal is:

- Faithfulness
- Clarity
- Representation

This frees the believer from a burden he was never meant to carry. We are not called to control outcomes or guarantee approval. We are called to represent Christ faithfully. Once that becomes settled in the heart, rejection loses some of its power. The believer no longer treats negative responses as proof that he should have remained silent. He understands that obedience is measured by faithfulness, not by universal acceptance.

The Power of a Decided Life

There is something powerful about a believer who has decided:

- I will not withdraw
- I will not remain silent
- I will not compromise

That decision changes:

- Behavior
- Presence
- Impact

Some changes in spiritual life do not begin with emotion. They begin with a decision. There is a holy firmness that forms when the believer settles certain matters before God. Once withdrawal is no longer an option in the heart, life begins to stand differently. The atmosphere around that person may not change immediately, but that person's posture does. And often, posture is where influence begins.

From Occasional to Intentional

Many believers engage occasionally. But influence requires intentional living.

Meaning:

- Thinking ahead
- Being prepared
- Recognizing opportunities

Occasional faithfulness is not enough for sustained influence. A believer must become watchful and awake. Intentional living means carrying readiness into the day. It means not drifting through conversations half-conscious of an assignment. It means learning to anticipate the moments where truth, grace, courage, and clarity may be needed, and being willing to meet them with purpose.

The Responsibility of Knowledge

Now that you know, you are accountable because knowledge increases responsibility.

You can no longer say, "I didn't know."

Now you must decide, "Will I act?"

This is where truth becomes weighty in a good and holy way. God does not reveal things merely to expand the mind. He reveals how they shape life. Once a believer has seen clearly, he cannot remain as passive as before without feeling the tension of disobedience. That tension is not cruelty. It is mercy. It is God refusing to let revelation become decoration instead of transformation.

Luke 12:48 says, "For everyone to whom much is given, from him much will be required" (NKJV). Spiritual understanding always carries holy responsibility with it.

The World Is Not Waiting for Perfect Believers

You may feel:

- Unready
- Incomplete
- Still growing

That is normal.

But the world is not waiting for perfection. It is waiting for:

- Willingness
- Clarity
- Presence

This line matters because many believers postpone obedience until they imagine a future version of themselves who feels more complete, more prepared, more confident, and less human. But much of God's work in our lives happens while we are still growing. He does not wait for polished people. He works through willing ones. What the world often needs most is not flawless representation, but honest, available, and Spirit-led faithfulness.

God Works through Available People

You do not need to:

- Have all the answers
- Be fully developed
- Be flawless

You need to:

- Be available
- Be intentional
- Be responsive

Availability is one of the most overlooked strengths in the Christian life. God can teach the teachable, guide the responsive, and strengthen the willing. The believer who stays available before God often becomes far more useful than the believer who is always waiting to feel complete before obeying. Availability keeps the heart open. It makes room for growth while still allowing obedience to begin now.

A Turning Point

This chapter is your turning point:

- From observer
  to participant
- From passive
  to intentional
- From avoidance
  to influence

Turning points are rarely dramatic on the outside at first. Often, they are quiet decisions made before God. But those decisions carry great power because they redirect one's life. The believer stops standing at the edge of what he knows and finally steps into what he has been shown. This is where truth stops being admired and starts being embodied.

A Personal Decision

Right now, the question is simple: will you continue as you were, or will you step into what you are called to be?

This question is deeply personal because no one else can answer it for you. Encouragement can point you forward. Teaching can strengthen you. Scripture can illuminate the path. But eventually, you must choose whether your life will remain governed by hesitation or surrendered to assignment.

A Final Charge

You have:

- The identity
- The understanding

- The model
- The tools

Now:

- Step in
- Speak up
- Act with purpose

Do not wait for all fear to disappear before you move. Do not wait for a perfect environment before you obey. Do not wait for some future version of yourself before you become useful to God. The grace of God meets believers in movement. As you step, He strengthens. As you obey, He teaches. As you engage, He forms.

Points to Ponder

1. Where have I been avoiding engagement?
2. What opportunities have I missed due to fear or hesitation?
3. What needs to change in my mindset?
4. What is one area where I will begin to act?
5. Have I been comforting myself with understanding while resisting the obedience that understanding requires?
6. What part of my life most clearly reveals the gap between what I know and what I am actually doing?
7. Where is God asking me to stop observing and start participating with courage and intention?

Call to Action

Choose one specific area this week:

- A conversation
- A relationship
- An environment

And step in with intention. Do not wait for perfect conditions. Act now.

Before you step in, pray clearly and simply. Ask the Lord to govern your heart, purify your motives, and steady your spirit. Then take one deliberate action that reflects obedience instead of hesitation. Keep it practical. Keep it real. Let this week mark a visible shift from delay to movement.

Declaration

I move from avoidance to influence. I am intentional, courageous, and prepared. I do not shrink back, I step forward. My life carries purpose in every environment. I will speak, act, and represent with clarity and conviction. Through me, God's light will shine.

I reject every habit of passivity that has made my witness smaller than my calling. What God has taught me will not remain hidden in me; it will become visible through me. I am not merely informed, I am being sent, and I will respond with obedience.

Prayer

Father,

Thank you for everything you have shown me. Now give me the courage to act. Remove every hesitation and fear. Help me to step into my assignment with confidence. Teach me to live intentionally and represent You well. Let my life move from passive to impactful.

Lord, take everything You have been teaching me and make it alive in my daily walk. Do not let truth remain stored in me without fruit. Break every pattern of delay, every excuse that sounds wise but hides fear, and every habit of hesitation that keeps me from stepping into obedience. Teach me to recognize the moments You place before me and to respond with courage, humility, and clarity. Let my life become steady proof that Your Word does not only inform me, it transforms me. Make me present where I used to withdraw, clear where I used to remain silent, and faithful where I once remained passive. From this day forward, I choose to engage.

In Jesus' name,

Amen.

Chapter 17: Raising Confident Believers

Why the Church Must Equip, Not Just Inspire

This chapter turns the focus toward the responsibility of formation. It is not enough for believers to be moved emotionally, stirred spiritually, or encouraged temporarily. They must also be prepared. A church may be full of sincere people and still leave many of them vulnerable if it does not intentionally train them for life beyond the sanctuary.

What follows is both a challenge and an invitation: the Church must recover the work of equipping believers so that faith can remain strong not only in worship, but also in the world.

If believers are:

- Afraid to engage
- Unable to explain
- Unprepared to stand

Then we must ask an honest question: where did the breakdown happen?

Because believers do not become passive by accident. They are often:

- Under-equipped
- Under-trained
- Under-challenged

That diagnosis is deeply important. Too often, passivity is treated as though it were only a personal weakness, when in many cases it is also the fruit of incomplete formation. A believer may genuinely love God and still remain uncertain in moments that require clarity, because no one ever helped him build that strength intentionally. This is why the issue is not merely individual failure. It is also a discipleship issue.

Inspiration without Equipping Is Incomplete

Many churches are strong in:

- Worship
- Preaching
- Encouragement

But weak in:

- Training
- Equipping
- Developing believers for real-world engagement

So people leave inspired, but not equipped. And when real-life challenges come, they struggle.

This is one of the quiet weaknesses of modern church culture. Inspiration can lift the heart for a moment, but if it is not joined to formation, it may not survive the pressures of Monday morning. A person can leave a service moved, strengthened emotionally, and full of good desire, yet still feel unprepared when faced with hard questions, opposing beliefs, moral complexity, or demanding environments. Encouragement matters, but encouragement alone does not always create readiness.

The Church must not choose between inspiration and equipping. It must offer both. One warms the heart. The other strengthens life. Together, they help produce believers who are not only touched by truth but also built by it.

The Responsibility of Leadership

Leaders are not only called to gather people. They are called to prepare people.

"To equip the saints for the work of ministry…", Ephesians 4:12

And ministry is not limited to the pulpit.

It includes:

- The workplace
- Society
- Daily interactions

This is a needed correction in how many believers think about ministry. Ministry is not reserved for a microphone, a stage, or a church building. It happens wherever Christ must be represented, in homes, offices, schools, neighborhoods, systems, and conversations. If leaders only prepare believers for church activity and not for public witness, then much of the believer's real assignment remains unsupported.

Ephesians 4:12, NKJV, reminds us that leaders are given *"for the equipping of the saints for the work of ministry."* That means leadership is not complete when people gather well. It becomes fruitful when people are prepared to live faithfully beyond the gathering.

What Must Be Taught?

If we want confident believers, we must intentionally teach:

1. Identity

- Who they are in Christ
- What they carry
- Where they stand

Without identity, everything else collapses.

Identity remains foundational because insecurity weakens everything else. A believer who does not know who he is before God will struggle to remain stable when challenged by people, culture, or pressure. He may have the right doctrine in fragments, yet still lack the inward steadiness needed to carry it with peace. Identity anchors the soul before public engagement ever begins.

2. Understanding

- Why they believe
- How to explain their faith
- How to think clearly

Without understanding, confidence is fragile.

This is essential because unexplained faith often becomes intimidated faith. Believers must not only feel truth; they must also understand it enough to express it. Clarity gives structure to conviction. It helps a believer move from vague sincerity to thoughtful representation. And when understanding grows, panic often begins to lose its grip.

3. Engagement Skills

- How to listen
- How to respond
- How to handle opposition

Without these, believers avoid conversations.

These skills matter because conviction alone does not always teach a person how to move through a real conversation wisely. Many believers know what they believe, yet still do not know how to remain calm, how to ask good questions, how to speak with grace, or how to stay present when resistance appears. Engagement is not only about content. It is also about posture, wisdom, and steadiness.

4. Practical Application

- Faith in money
- Faith in justice
- Faith in systems

Without application, faith remains theoretical.

The Church must not stop at abstract truth. Believers need help applying the Kingdom to the practical arenas of life. If faith remains beautiful in concept but disconnected from money, power, justice, relationships, responsibility, and daily decisions, then it has not yet matured into full usefulness. Truth must become livable, not merely admirable.

We Must Train for Real Life, Not Just Church Life

Many believers are prepared for church environments, but not for real-world conversations, such as:

- Challenging questions
- Complex situations

This must change because most of their lives happen outside the church walls.

This sentence carries tremendous weight. Most believers will spend far more time in the world than in a church gathering. That means the greater part of discipleship must prepare them for where they actually live, work, think, struggle, and represent Christ. A church may do many things well and still leave its people unready if it forms them only for internal participation and not for external witness.

Jesus never trained His followers only for private circles of agreement. He prepared them for crowds, questions, misunderstandings, spiritual resistance, and public mission. The Church must do the same if it wants to build believers who can remain faithful in real life.

A Shift in Church Culture

Church must move from:

- "Come and receive."

to:

- "Come and be prepared to go."

Because the goal is not attendance, the goal is transformation and deployment.

This shift is not against gathering. It gives gathering its fuller purpose. We come together not only to receive comfort, but to be strengthened for the mission. We are gathered so we may be formed, and formed so we may be sent. When this becomes part of church culture, believers stop seeing church as a spiritual shelter from the world alone and start seeing it as a place of preparation for faithful presence within the world.

Safe Spaces vs. Strong Believers

There is value in safe environments. But if believers only grow in:

- Comfort
- Agreement
- Familiarity

They will struggle in:

- Opposition
- Tension
- Diversity of thought

We must build strong believers, not just comfortable ones.

Comfort has its place, especially in healing, restoration, and encouragement. But comfort cannot become the highest goal of discipleship. If believers are only nurtured where nothing pushes against them, then they may remain tender but untested, sincere but unstable, comforted but not courageous. The Church must care for people deeply while also preparing them honestly.

A strong believer is not one who becomes harsh, loud, or self-assured in the flesh. A strong believer is one who can remain rooted in Christ when familiarity disappears. That kind of strength does not come from constant ease. It comes from intentional formation.

Encouraging Questions, Not Silencing Them

A healthy church:

- Welcomes questions
- Encourages thinking
- Creates space for discussion

Because when questions are:

- Ignored
- Dismissed

believers will:

- Seek answers elsewhere
- Or remain confused

This is especially important in a generation surrounded by competing voices. If the Church becomes a place where sincere questions feel unwelcome, many believers will either hide their uncertainty or search for clarity in places that do not honor truth. Neither outcome is healthy. But when churches create space for thoughtful, honest engagement, they become places where conviction can deepen instead of remaining shallow.

God is not threatened by sincere inquiry. Truth does not weaken when examined carefully. In many cases, healthy questioning is one of the very ways believers grow beyond borrowed language into personal conviction.

Modeling Matters

Leaders must:

- Demonstrate engagement
- Show how to respond
- Live what they teach

Because people learn more from:

- What they see

than from:

- What they hear

This is a powerful reminder that discipleship is embodied. Believers watch how leaders handle pressure, disagreement, difficult people, and challenging environments. They notice whether those who teach truth also know how to carry it calmly, courageously, and humanly. A leader who models steady engagement often teaches more deeply than a leader who only speaks about it in theory.

Paul captured this pattern when he said, *"Imitate me, just as I also imitate Christ"* (1 Corinthians 11:1, NKJV). The life of the teacher becomes part of the teaching itself.

The Next Generation Is Watching

Younger believers are asking:

- "Is my faith real in the world?"
- "Can it stand in today's culture?"
- "Does it actually work outside church?"

If we do not answer these questions, they will find answers elsewhere.

These are not rebellious questions. They are urgent ones. Younger believers are not merely asking whether Christianity is beautiful in church settings. They want to know whether it can remain true under pressure, credible in public life, and strong in a complex world. If the Church does not help them connect faith to reality, then other voices will eagerly step in to do that for them, often without truth, without grace, and without the mind of Christ.

This is why raising confident believers is not only about the present Church. It is also about the future witness of the gospel through the generations still coming.

Confidence Comes from Preparation

Confidence is not personality. It is preparation.

When believers are trained:

- They speak with clarity
- They engage without fear
- They stand with conviction

This matters because some believers assume confidence belongs only to naturally bold people. But biblical confidence is not merely temperamental. It is often the fruit of preparation, formation, and repeated obedience. A quiet believer who is well-grounded may stand more steadily than a loud believer who has never been deeply formed. Confidence built through preparation is often calmer, cleaner, and more durable than confidence built on personality alone.

Repetition Builds Strength

This cannot be a one-time message. It must be:

- Repeated
- Practiced
- Reinforced

Because growth requires consistency.

Truth deepens through repetition. Skills are strengthened through practice. Confidence grows through continued exposure and obedience. The Church must understand that one sermon on boldness, one class on apologetics, or one emotional moment of motivation will not by itself build resilient believers. Formation requires rhythm. It requires returning to truth until truth begins to shape instinct, reaction, and daily living.

A Culture of Growth

The Church must create a culture where:

- Learning is continuous
- Growth is expected
- Engagement is normal

Not optional.

This kind of culture changes everything. It teaches believers that discipleship is not a one-time experience, but a continual becoming. It normalizes development. It removes shame from growth. It reminds people that they do not have to stay where they are, and it calls them lovingly toward maturity. In such a culture, engagement stops feeling like a special assignment for a few bold believers and becomes part of the normal life of following Jesus.

From Consumers to Contributors

Many believers have been conditioned to receive, but not contribute.

We must shift them into:

- Active participants
- Engaged representatives

This is one of the most needed shifts in the modern Church. A consumer mindset asks only, *"What am I receiving?"* But a Kingdom mindset also asks, *"How am I growing, serving, representing, and strengthening others?"* The believer was never meant to remain a passive observer of spiritual things. He was called to become a living vessel through whom truth, grace, and light move outward.

A Personal Responsibility

While leadership must equip, each believer must take responsibility for growth.

You cannot depend entirely on others.

You must:

- Study
- Practice
- Engage

This chapter rightly places responsibility on both the Church and the individual believer. Leaders must equip, but believers must respond. No one grows by proximity alone. At some point, each believer must decide to pursue understanding, to practice what is learned, and to remain engaged enough for growth to become real. Spiritual maturity requires partnership with what God is providing.

Paul told Timothy, *"Be diligent to present yourself approved to God"* (2 Timothy 2:15, NKJV). That diligence belongs to the believer personally.

Multiplication Is the Goal

A confident believer should:

- Help others grow
- Teach what they have learned
- Reproduce strength in others

Because the goal is not addition, it is multiplication.

This is where maturity becomes fruitful. The believer who has been strengthened should not stop with personal improvement alone. He should become a source of strength to others. What has been learned should be shared. What has been gained should be multiplied. The Church becomes stronger when growth is not hoarded but reproduced.

2 Timothy 2:2 reflects this beautifully: *"the things that you have heard from me... commit these to faithful men who will be able to teach others also"* (NKJV). That is the rhythm of multiplication.

A Final Challenge to Leaders and Believers

Leaders equip intentionally. Believers grow actively because a strong Church is made of strong individuals.

This final challenge brings the chapter into sharp focus. The future strength of the Church will not be built only on attendance, activity, or inspiration. It will be built on believers who are formed deeply enough to stand, think clearly enough to explain, and engage maturely enough to represent Christ in the world. That kind of Church does not happen by accident. It is built through intentional leadership and responsive believers.

Points to Ponder

1. Am I equipped to engage the world confidently?
2. What areas do I still need to grow in?
3. Am I actively pursuing growth, or remaining passive?
4. How can I help others grow as well?
5. Have I been inspired more than I have been equipped?
6. What part of my faith still feels strong in church settings but weak in real-life settings?
7. Am I willing to take personal responsibility for becoming the kind of believer this chapter describes?

Call to Action

This week:

- Identify one area where you need to grow
- Take one intentional step to develop it
- Share one insight with someone else

Make that step specific. It may be studying a question you have avoided, practicing how to explain your faith more clearly, asking a mature believer for guidance, or stepping into a conversation you would normally avoid. Then pass on one thing you learned. Let growth become both personal and multiplying.

Declaration

I am equipped, prepared, and growing. I take responsibility for my development. I am confident in my faith and clear in my understanding. I engage the world with wisdom and courage. I am not only growing, but I am helping others grow. Through me, strength will multiply.

I reject passive Christianity and embrace intentional formation. I will not remain underdeveloped where God is calling me to become strong. The Lord is shaping me into a believer who can stand, speak, serve, and strengthen others with faithfulness and clarity.

Prayer

Father,

Thank you for the opportunity to grow and be equipped. Help me take responsibility for my development. Give me a hunger for understanding and a desire to improve. Surround me with the right people and resources. Teach me not only to grow, but to help others grow. Let my life be a source of strength and clarity.

Lord, deliver me from every form of passive faith that waits to be carried instead of choosing to mature. Deepen my roots in You. Strengthen the places where I am still uncertain, untrained, or hesitant. Give me a heart that welcomes growth, a mind that pursues truth, and a spirit that remains teachable. Help me receive what faithful leaders offer, but also help me respond with discipline, obedience, and intention. Let my life become proof that Your Church is not only a place of encouragement, but a place of formation. And as You strengthen me, make me able to strengthen others with humility, wisdom, and love.

In Jesus' name,

Amen.

Chapter 18: A Call To Engage The World

You Were Not Saved to Withdraw, You Were Sent to Transform

This chapter carries the weight of response. By now, the path has been made plain. What was once uncertain has been named, explained, and brought into the light. But understanding alone is never the final destination of truth. Truth always reaches for embodiment. It asks the believer not only to agree, but to move. Not only to admire conviction, but to carry it into daily life. This chapter is a summons to that movement.

There comes a moment when everything becomes clear, not just in understanding, but in responsibility. You have now seen:

- Who you are
- What you carry
- How Jesus lived
- What is expected

The question is no longer, *"What does this mean?"* The question is, *"What will I do now?"*

That is the question every mature believer must eventually face. There comes a point when more explanation is no longer what we need most. We need obedience. We need a response. We need the courage to let truth leave the page, leave the private moment, leave the safe place, and enter the visible parts of life. This is often where spiritual growth becomes costly, but also where it becomes beautiful.

The Time of Passive Faith Is Over

You can no longer:

- Hide behind uncertainty
- Remain silent out of fear
- Withdraw into comfort

Because now you know:

- You are light
- You are sent
- You are responsible

That language is strong, but it is necessary. Responsibility is one of the clearest signs of real spiritual maturity. Once God has shown us what He has shown us, passivity becomes harder to justify. The believer who knows he is light cannot keep treating silence as neutrality. The believer who knows he is sent cannot keep calling withdrawal wisdom when God is clearly asking for presence.

"To him who knows to do good and does not do it, to him it is sin" (James 4:17, NKJV). That verse is not meant to crush the heart, but to awaken it. Knowing carries responsibility.

The World You See Is Not Random

The confusion, the tension, the opposing views, they are not accidents.

They are:

- Opportunities
- Open doors
- Invitations for engagement

This changes the way the believer reads the world around him. He stops seeing difficulty only as an interruption and begins to recognize that many of the very things he once feared may actually be the places where God intends his witness to become useful. Tension may be uncomfortable, but it also reveals need. Opposition may be exhausting, but it also reveals where clarity is absent. The believer must learn to see beyond discomfort and into the assignment.

You Carry What the World Needs

The world has:

- Information
- Opinions
- Voices

But it is lacking:

- Clarity
- Truth

- Stability

And that is what you carry.

This should settle deeply in the heart. The believer is not empty-handed in the world. He is not entering confusion with nothing to offer. He carries the truth of Christ, the stabilizing power of identity, the wisdom of Scripture, and the witness of a life that has been touched by grace. That is not a small thing. In an age filled with noise, confusion, and instability, the clear truth carried with love becomes deeply precious.

Jesus said, *"You are the salt of the earth"* and *"You are the light of the world"* (Matthew 5:13–14, NKJV). He did not describe believers as optional ornaments in history. He described them as a necessary presence.

Stop Waiting for the Perfect Moment

Many believers are waiting for:

- The right time
- The right situation
- The right level of confidence

But influence does not begin with perfection. It begins with a decision.

That is where many delays must finally be confronted. The perfect moment is often a disguised excuse. The believer waits until he feels stronger, clearer, calmer, more complete, more certain, and somehow less human. But real obedience rarely begins in ideal emotional conditions. It begins when the heart says yes to God before the emotions fully catch up.

Engagement Is a Daily Choice

Every day, you will face moments where you must decide:

- Speak or stay silent
- Engage or withdraw
- Act or ignore

And in those moments, your decision determines your impact.

You Will Not Feel Ready, Act Anyway

Let's be honest. You may still feel:

- Incomplete
- Uncertain
- Still growing

That is normal.

But readiness does not come before action. It comes through action.

This is one of the most freeing truths in the chapter. Many believers imagine readiness as something they must fully possess before obedience begins. But often, God forms readiness in the process of obedience itself. We learn by engaging. We grow by stepping in. We mature by responding. The believer who waits to feel fully prepared may remain waiting far longer than God intended.

Whoever fears to act because he is not fully formed will often remain unformed in the very place where obedience was meant to shape him.

Your Presence Matters

Where you are matters.

Who you interact with matters.

What you say matters.

Because you carry influence whether you realize it or not.

This is a holy reminder that daily life is never as small as it seems. The believer's presence is not meaningless. His words are not neutral. His posture, integrity, faithfulness, and courage all leave traces. Sometimes we do not see immediately what our presence has done in a room, a relationship, or a difficult moment. But heaven sees it. And often, the fruit of faithful presence appears later than we expect.

The Cost of Silence

Every time you remain silent, avoid engagement, or hold back the truth, something is lost.

Not just for you, but for someone who needed:

- Clarity
- Direction
- Truth

That is why silence must be examined with seriousness. Not every quiet moment is wrong, but many silences are not harmless. Sometimes what is lost is unseen by us in the moment. A person may have needed one clear word. A relationship may have needed one faithful act. A confused mind may have needed one stable response. We may never fully know what our silence withheld. But God does, and that is why this chapter calls us beyond it.

You Are Not Alone in This Assignment

You are not sent alone. God:

- Goes with you
- Guides you
- Strengthens you

You are supported by:

- His Spirit
- His Word
- His presence

This is where courage finds its deepest source. The believer is not being pushed into public faithfulness with nothing but human effort. God goes with what He sends. His presence does not stop at the church door, the prayer closet, or the private moment. He remains with His people in conversations, in systems, in difficult environments, in opposition, in uncertainty, and in the ordinary places where witness must become visible.

"Lo, I am with you always, even to the end of the age" (Matthew 28:20, NKJV). The One who sends us also remains with us.

You Will Make Mistakes, Keep Moving

You will not say everything perfectly or handle every situation flawlessly. That is not the goal. Growth requires:

- Practice
- Adjustment
- Persistence

This protects the believer from another form of fear. The goal is not spotless performance. The goal is faithful movement. Mistakes may happen. Awkward moments may come. Some conversations may not go as hoped. But none of that should become permission to retreat. God often forms maturity through imperfect obedience that stays teachable and keeps going.

The Power of One Life Fully Engaged

One believer who is:

- Clear
- Confident
- Engaged

can:

- Influence many
- Change environments
- Shift perspectives

You do not need a platform. You need willingness.

This is one of the most encouraging truths in the chapter. Influence is not reserved for the famous, the visible, or the publicly celebrated. It belongs to willing believers who carry Christ sincerely where they are. One life rooted in God, steady in truth, and awake to assignment can affect far more than it realizes. That kind of life becomes a witness not by spectacle, but by faithful presence.

"Let no one despise your youth, but be an example to the believers" (1 Timothy 4:12, NKJV). Influence begins where example and willingness meet.

A Generation Must Rise

A generation of believers who:

- Know who they are
- Understand what they believe
- Engage without fear
- Speak with clarity
- Live with integrity

This is what is needed now.

This is not only a personal call. It is a generational one. The hour demands believers who are not easily shaken, not hidden behind fear, and not content with private sincerity alone. It demands men and women whose faith has become clear enough to stand, human enough to reach people, and strong enough to remain present in a complicated world. This is the generation the Spirit of God is still able to raise.

The Final Shift

- From learning
  to living
- From understanding
  to action
- From avoidance
  to influence

This is the great movement of the book's burden. The believer is no longer meant to remain a careful observer of truth. He is being called into embodiment, into visible faithfulness, into daily witness, into courageous movement. This shift is where everything previously taught begins to gather itself into one practical response.

Your Assignment Begins Now

Not tomorrow. Not later. Now.

In your conversations. In your environment. In your daily life.

That word *now* matters. It breaks the illusion that obedience belongs only to some future season. Your assignment is not waiting for a dramatic opening. It has already begun in the place where you live, where you work, where you speak, where you notice, where you decide, and where you remain available to God.

A Personal Charge

Wherever you go:

- Be aware
- Be intentional
- Be ready

Do not blend in. Stand firm. Speak clearly.

This charge is simple, but full of weight. Awareness means you no longer drift through life unconsciously. Intentionality means you stop treating your daily environment as random. Readiness means your heart remains available to God. Standing firm means your convictions stay rooted. Speaking clearly means what God has formed in you no longer remains hidden when truth is needed.

Points to Ponder

1. Where am I still waiting for a "better time" to obey?
2. What daily moments am I overlooking that may actually be part of my assignment?
3. When I feel unready, do I delay obedience or move forward in trust?
4. Is my silence protecting comfort, or withholding truth from someone who needs it?
5. Have I allowed understanding to comfort me without allowing it to send me?
6. What part of my life is God already asking me to engage more intentionally right now?
7. If I truly believed my assignment begins now, what would change this week in how I move, speak, and respond?

Call to Action

This week, choose one ordinary area of your life and treat it as a holy assignment:

- A conversation
- A recurring relationship
- A workplace moment
- A setting you usually move through without much awareness

Go into it prayerfully and intentionally. Do not wait to feel fully ready. Do not wait for perfect conditions. Step in as one who is sent.

Before you enter that moment, pause and pray with simplicity: *"Lord, help me to be aware, faithful, clear, and available here."* Then watch closely. Listen carefully. Speak when needed. Let one ordinary space become the place where your obedience becomes visible.

Declaration

I am not called to hide, I am called to engage. I am sent by God, and my life carries purpose. I do not wait for perfect conditions to obey. I move with courage, clarity, and intention. My presence matters, my voice matters, and my obedience matters. Through me, truth, stability, and light will be carried into the world.

I reject every delay that has disguised itself as preparation when God is calling me to move now. I am not empty-handed in this generation; I carry what Christ has placed within me. I will live awake to assignment, steady in identity, and willing in obedience.

Prayer

Father,

Thank you for everything you have shown me. Thank You for not only revealing the truth, but also calling me to live it. Forgive me for every place where I have delayed obedience, waited for a better moment, or hidden behind the feeling of being unready.

Teach me to live as one who is sent. Make me aware in my daily life. Make me intentional in my choices. Make me courageous in moments where truth is needed. Help me stop treating ordinary life as spiritually small. Let me see my conversations, my relationships, and my environments through the eyes of the assignment. Strengthen me when I feel uncertain. Guide me when I do not know exactly what to do. Keep me steady when fear tries to make me withdraw.

Lord, raise me into the kind of believer this chapter calls for, present, clear, faithful, and willing. Let Your Spirit make me more responsive than hesitant, more available than guarded, and more obedient than delayed. Teach me to trust that You go with me into every place You send me. And let my life, in all its ordinary moments, become a visible witness that I was not saved to retreat, but sent to bring light, truth, and holy influence wherever I go.

In Jesus' name,

Amen.

Epilogue, When Light Stops Hiding

There comes a moment in every believer's life when truth must become more than something admired. It must become something lived. That is the burden of this book.

Not merely that we would understand the world better. Not merely that we would identify the fear, the silence, the hesitation, and the weakness. But that we would rise from them. Because the greatest tragedy is not that darkness exists. Darkness has always existed.

The tragedy is when light forgets itself. The tragedy is when those who have been called, filled, taught, and sent begin to live as though they were made only for safety, only for private devotion, only for the comfort of agreement. That is not the life Jesus modeled, and it is not the life He died to give us.

He did not redeem us so we could hide in religious language while the world groans for truth. He did not save us so we could remain spiritually alive but publicly absent. He did not call us out of darkness simply to become careful observers of the light.

He called us to shine.

And shining is not passive. It is visible. It is costly. It is often uncomfortable. It requires clarity. It requires courage. It requires a heart that has become settled enough in God that it no longer needs the constant protection of safe environments in order to remain faithful.

This is why the journey of this book matters so deeply.

We have seen that fear is often rooted in uncertainty. We have seen that silence often grows where identity is weak. We have seen that many believers love God sincerely, yet remain underprepared to explain, engage, and influence. We have seen that holiness was never meant to become isolation, and that Christian community was never meant to become containment. We have seen that faith must move beyond private inspiration and become public representation.

We have seen that transformed people can affect structures, systems, conversations, and culture. And above all, we have seen that Jesus is still the model, clear, holy, present, courageous, and unafraid.

Now the question is not whether these things are true. The question is whether they will become true in us. Will we continue to admire boldness from a distance, or will we become believers who step forward?

Will we keep waiting for the perfect moment, or will we recognize that much of our assignment is already in front of us?

Will we continue to protect ourselves from discomfort, or will we allow the Spirit of God to make us steady enough to remain present where truth is needed most?

These questions are not small. They are the difference between a faith that comforts only the believer and a faith that blesses the world around him. They are the difference between private conviction and public witness. They are the difference between light that exists and light that shines.

The times we are living in do not need a Church that is merely louder. They need a Church that is clearer.

They need believers who know who they are, know what they believe, know how to speak, know how to stand, and know how to remain full of both grace and truth.

They need Christians whose holiness has not made them unreachable, and whose compassion has not made them vague. They need sons and daughters of God who have become spiritually deep, intellectually awake, emotionally steady, and practically useful.

That kind of believer is still possible. That kind of Church is still possible. And perhaps more than ever, that kind of witness is necessary now.

So let this not end as a book that was simply read.

Let it become a mirror. Let it become a call. Let it become a turning point. Let it challenge every place where fear has made you small. Let it expose every place where comfort has replaced calling. Let it awaken every place where your voice has been hidden under hesitation. Let it remind you that your life is not random, your presence is not meaningless, and your faith was never meant to remain trapped inside church walls, safe circles, or private thoughts.

You were sent.

Sent into conversations.

Sent into relationships.

Sent into workplaces.

Sent into systems.

Sent into communities.

Sent into ordinary days that heaven can still fill with extraordinary purpose.

And if you are sent, then you are not stranded in this generation.

You are placed.

You are trusted.

You are responsible.

So walk as one who knows. Stand as one who belongs to God. Speak as one who has been taught by truth. Love as one who has encountered grace. And shine as one who has finally stopped apologizing for being light in a dark world.

Because in the end, darkness is not defeated by those who study light from a distance. It is confronted by those who carry it within.

Dr. Jean Heder Petit-Frere

Final Conclusion

This book began with a problem: believers who are called to be light, yet often feel uncomfortable in darkness.

It ends with a summons: become what you have already been called to be.

The answer has never been more withdrawal. The answer has never been safer silence. The answer has never been a smaller Christianity hidden inside familiar spaces.

The answer is identity.

The answer is understanding.

The answer is spiritual maturity.

The answer is courageous engagement shaped by the life of Jesus Christ.

When identity is clear, fear begins to lose its grip. When understanding deepens, silence begins to break. When faith becomes steady, engagement becomes possible. When believers stop hiding, influence begins. That is the heartbeat of everything written here.

You do not need to become someone else. You do not need a perfect personality. You do not need flawless answers. You do not need a public platform.

You need to surrender.

You need growth.

You need courage.

You need willingness.

You need the settled confidence that comes from knowing whose you are and why you have been sent.

The world is not waiting for perfect Christians. It is waiting for faithful ones.

Faithful in truth.

Faithful in tone.

Faithful in presence.

Faithful in courage.

Faithful in the ordinary places where witness often begins.

So as this book closes, let your life open. Let your worship become witness. Let your convictions become visible. Let your learning become living. Let your faith become strong enough to remain present in the places where God has assigned you.

- Do not retreat.
- Do not blend in.
- Do not keep postponing the obedience that God is already calling for now.
- Be clear.
- Be grounded.
- Be gracious.
- Be courageous.
- Be present.
- And wherever God has placed you, carry Christ there well.